Twyford's Valiant Hearts

Twyford's Valiant Hearts

Twyford Men Lost in the First World War

Twyford's First World War Remembrance Project

A Community Project Researching the Lives of the Men from Twyford, Hampshire commemorated on the First World War Memorial in the Church of St Mary the Virgin

Edited by Christopher Pope

Published by The Twyford Historical Society,
Twyford, Hampshire, England

First published 2018, First Edition

A Project in conjunction with the Imperial War Museum and supported by Hampshire County Council

ISBN: 978-1-9996050-0-1

Printed and bound by Doxzoo in the UK at High Wycombe

Front Cover Illustration: High Street, Twyford
looking North from the junction with Park Lane

Back cover illustration copyright © St Mary's Church PCC, Twyford

FIRST WORLD WAR CENTENARY LED BY IWM

Hampshire County Council

Contents

1. INTRODUCTION 1
   - Our Remembrance Project 1
   - The Life of a Twyford Lad in 1910 4
   - "For King and Country", August 1914: Why did so many sign up? 7
2. TWYFORD'S WAR MEMORIAL 10
3. THE MEN ON THE MEMORIAL 13
   - The Mussell Brothers, Chas Frederick and Sydney A 13
   - Lennox Dutton Shrimpton 17
   - William Light 23
   - Frederick Robt Brown 25
   - Leonard H A Herridge 30
   - Frank Henry J Dumper 35
   - Alfred J Higgins 41
   - Geo Rainier Crawford 44
   - The Webb Brothers, Mark and Walter George 50
   - Jack Stanley Powell 59
   - Thomas Mostyn Field 64
   - Geo William Hadley 71
   - Walter Chas C Cox 75
   - Edwin Platt 79
   - George Mansell 84
   - Walter Shave 91
   - Walter Chas H Feltham 96
   - George Collins 99
   - Wm James Barnes 104
   - William Eades 107
   - Thomas Wm Knight 111
   - Herbert Tring Sapsed 119
   - Albert Chas Hickman 124
   - Bruce Hutchinson Campbell 127
   - Henry P Parrott 135
   - Ernest Reason 137
   - Percy F J Allen 141
4. THE MEN IN THE CHURCHYARD 144
   - Walter George Dale 144
   - John Douglas Small 148
   - Alfred Carpenter 151

5. LIFE IN THE VILLAGE 156
Belgian Refugees in Twyford, 1914 156
Twyford Parish in the First World War 159
Hazeley Down Camp 163
Twyford Bells – Their Message 171
6. AFTERWORD - Impact on the Village 172
7. APPENDICES 176
Twyford's Roll of Honour 176
Contributors to the Project 177
Parish Hall Boards 178
Bible Class Roll of Honour 179
Photograph Acknowledgements 180
Map of Twyford in 1910 181

1. INTRODUCTION

Our Remembrance Project

In the summer of 2013 a number of us in Twyford considered what we could do in the village to mark the centenary of the First World War. Conscious that our war memorial bore 29 names, we realised that we knew very little about these men. A spur to us was provided by our neighbouring village of Owslebury where the church contained an impressive display of key facts and background for each man on their honour roll.

And so we decided to investigate our 29 names and try to assemble their stories to enable us to say that Twyford had honoured the words of Laurence Binyon, "We will remember them".

An open meeting was called to see what support there was to develop the idea of 'Twyford's First World War Remembrance Project'. From the outset some 20 people were involved with many prepared to contribute their time and skills. So we developed the idea as community local history project, sharing out the men named on the roll to individual present-day villagers to conduct research on 'their' men, and as we established, boys, and to write their stories. The journey for many of us was not always easy; we had significant skills to master in using computers to research family histories and in appreciating the military significances of the time as they applied to our men. In part as a result of this the project took much longer than we had anticipated. However we had determined to produce stories for the men and boys that would be readable and interesting to our friends and fellow villagers, both current and future, and the two years planned grew to five.

As our research developed, we got closer to these men. After all they had trodden the same paths and lanes as we ourselves, lived in the same houses, been to the same school, used 'our' post office, were baptised, married and worshipped at the same church, but, because of the war, had been denied a final resting place in our churchyard. In two cases we traced relatives of the men still living in the village, and we were successful in reaching out to several others, who contributed to the stories. We have tried to understand the military units they joined, their immediate history before our men were killed and the circumstances that led to their deaths.

We had occasional meetings to inform ourselves and prepare for the research process, sharing useful internet/web sites, experiences of our County Records Office and copies of regimental archives and war diaries we had discovered.

Of course we received much help, not least from those now long gone. Our village has published a monthly magazine since 1899 and this proved a valuable resource for the war years; Miss Leila Hull, who enjoys near iconic status in our village, established a Bible Reading Class over a hundred years ago that nurtured many of the young men and boys at that time. She left us a photo album and scrap book, with correspondence with many of the village's young soldiers, that has been a terrific source. I would also mention the decision taken in 1919/20 to include on our war memorial not just the surnames of the fallen, but their full names, rank, ship or army unit and year of death. This gives us confidence that in our searches of registers, indexes, databases and the internet we have identified the correct man. [For the many village memorials bearing just christian and surnames that one has seen, the exercise we have conducted would, I suspect, not have been realistic.] Another recent development, release of the 1911 Census data under the 100-year rule, gave us access to an enormous amount of detail on the eve of the outbreak of war about our village and the people we were researching.

Our village has been fortunate in having our parish registers committed to digital form and published on the internet, making their access simple and effective.

Our stories developed as the number of them increased over the years and many also acquired their own distinctive character dependent on their author's interests and style. We have decided not to edit these out into a single apparent style; please read each story as an individual offering from one of today's Twyfordians as they have discovered and understood more about one of their predecessors.

We determined to use the medium of our Parish Magazine to publish the stories initially and the first of these appeared in February 2014. The stories then continued at roughly monthly intervals to the end of 2016. We then realised that we should include the three additional First World War casualties buried in our churchyard, who for various reasons do not appear on the Twyford memorial; these stories appeared in 2017, giving us a total of 32 stories. The general interest in the war years also resulted in several other complementary pieces about the village during the war which are included.

The starting point for our journey was the War Memorial. This volume reflects this in showing the names of the men as they appear on the memorial at each section heading and their stories appear in what we now know to be date of death order. This has highlighted some apparent discrepancies as explained more fully below.

The sequence will enable the reader to form a view of the impact of the war on families at the time and the village as a whole as it progressed. In the case of brothers, they are treated together and appear here at the date of death of the first. For initial publication in our magazine, the stories appeared as their authors completed them and readers may need to make some allowance for this as they read them now in a different order.

Eagle-eyed readers may notice slight discrepancies in dates and ages of some of these men. In practice it has not proved possible to be absolutely certain about the ages at death of all of them. Birth certificates were not available for all, it was not an age when 'proof of ID' was required to join up and we have found numerous cases where incorrect particulars were supplied on census forms, join-up papers and other documentation. However the general richness of the data available and supporting material leaves us confident than we have the right men.

We are grateful for support from Hampshire County Council, from the 'Hampshire Commemorates: First World War and D-Day Grant Scheme 2013/2014'.

The Life of a Twyford Lad in 1910

The following story appeared in the Hampshire Chronicle circa 1955 by Edward 'Ted' Charles Hunt who, at the time of the 1911 Census, when he was 11, lived in Manor Cottages, Twyford, with his grandparents Alfred and Amelia Hunt. It gives a wonderful portrayal of life in our, perhaps not untypical, Hampshire village before the outbreak of the First World War and would have been an experience shared by very many of the young men who came to join up in the course of the war.

"Through an old Directory for Hampshire and the Isle of Wight I had a look back at the village of my boyhood days, Twyford. In 1910 it had a civil population of 1,479 and there were some forty gentlefolk who were still being driven around by their coachmen. The principle landowners were Major Bishop, Horace Trimmer and Mrs Conway Shipley who was the Lady of the Manor.

There were many farm men and lads following the plough on the farms of W F Maidment and his brother, also that of Mr J F Best of Hazeley, and a large number of sheep were also kept. The two Smithys, Carter & Son and William Thick were kept busy with so many horses to be shod and other iron work and the village lads would give a hand at striking with the large hammer after tea on winter nights. These lads always seemed to make their own amusements and thoroughly enjoy life. They used to whistle and sing more than they do today, although some of their homemade 'jingles' were sometimes not very complimentary. They sang of the barber Mr Stubbington:

'If you need to have a 'Stubby'
He will hover round your jaw
With a razor like a saw.'

The man of the law kept a wary eye on them; there were many washers and rounded pieces of lead in the chocolate machines on Shawford Station and there were parcels you could pick up on the road on moonlight nights only to have them snatched out of your grasp and see them fly over the hedge by means of long strings.

But at times they would put on 'pill box' hats, equipment, including a large buckled belt and shoulder a carbine. This was the Church Lads' Brigade who with a bugle band at their head would think nothing of a summer's evening march to Ghost's Corner, thence to Compton, Shawford and home.

Villages such as Twyford were fine places to live in back in those days. There was music through the village band and there was sport aplenty. At football, I first remember Twyford Juniors playing on a Hazeley Road pitch. I was a very small lad then and the very first time I went there a shot from a forward knocked me for six and I went home howling.

The St Mary's team played at Manor Farm field for some time and the Cricket club a few fields away where 'Buskit' and 'Bricky' Young were good all-rounders and Joe Unsworth a lusty hitter of fours and sixes. Sometimes the ball would land at a spot near the Itchen where small boys bathed in the nude.

Twyford St Mary's Primary School circa 1910

Editor's Note: I count 35 boy's faces in this photo. Perhaps Ted was one of these. This certainly constitutes one of the cohorts that was to be swept up into the war and some of our 'Valiant Hearts' may well be pictured here.

In addition to the present inns, there was the Scotch Ale House kept by William Hewett and Young & Co's brewery, where beer was sent out by horse dray at a price of 1s 4d per gallon.

One does not usually get mixed with religion but godspellers from the Soldiers Home Mission at Winchester were successful in holding experimental services at the Phoenix Inn, marching on dark evenings from Shawford Station with their band with acetylene lamps to light their way.

Doctor G A F Roberts was a very busy man being Medical Officer and public vaccinator. If your tooth ached you could visit his surgery where you would be asked not just to take a seat but to hold on to it. There was no gas or cocaine, it was a case of the more he pulled the more you 'hollered'.

There was one shop in Twyford I will never forget, a little Georgian shop with rounded windows. Here Henry William Hewett known as 'spot' carried on a saddler's business for around 60 years. His uncle and grandfather had worked there also. He also had a wonderful record as Churchwarden at St. Mary's Church.

My other recollections of Twyford include entertainment of various kinds, the fairs that used to park in front of the Bugle Inn with snake charmers, dancing girls and waxwork exhibitions. At the back of the Phoenix, the old showman from Waltham Chase, Jimmy Burchell, would give his one man band and shadow-graph show. 'Poor old Jimmy finished up bankrupt, they even sold his drum' a friend told me.

The Bugle Inn, circa 1912

I end this article with a story told me by my grandparents. A man and his wife in Twyford accused an old maid called Jane of theft, an accusation which was proved wrong. The villagers rose as one in wrath, formed a procession with a band to lead them and paraded effigies of them around the streets to the old toll gate cottage house at Manor Farm where they were placed on a bonfire in a field and burnt with Jane looking on in triumph.

Some years later there was another fire at this spot and this time it was a large straw rick. I ought to have known better, playing with matches at such a place; yes it was yours truly and three others. We deserved the birching that boys could get in those days but a kindly farmer forgave me."

Ted Hunt

"For King and Country", August 1914: Why did so many sign up?

In August 1914, 42 Twyford men signed up, in September another 37, in October another nine. By November, within three months of the declaration of war, this had risen to 90; all were volunteers. Not everyone was accepted; the rules were that you had to be 18 and under 38. Generally single men were preferred to married ones and you could be discharged if your wife objected. You also had to pass the fitness test. Forty per cent of the volunteers were rejected on medical grounds; this was a national figure which shocked the authorities who had to reduce standards as the war progressed. Much of this had to do with nutrition; country people however might be just as poor as those in the towns but had better food.

These 90 volunteers from Twyford represent about half the men in the 18 to 38 age group within the village. Analysis of the 1911 Census indicates Twyford's population was some 1,250, incorporating 600 males and that there were 184 men in this age bracket. Over the years of the war the number in the age bracket would have gone up or down as men rolled on, and off. If one were to rule out most of the married, the unfit and those in protected occupations, you will appreciate just how strong the pressure to volunteer was in those early days of the war, and how supportive was the response of this village to have achieved an almost 50% figure.

Who were these young men of Twyford who volunteered? If you want to know their names, they are all recorded in the Twyford Parish Magazines for September and October 1914 under the heading "Serving their King and Country"; "Twyford: 20th Century Chronicles" has the August intake on pp195 and 196[1]. If you want to know more about them, then the first place to look is the 1911 Census, which gives names, ages, residence, occupation and marital status of everyone in Twyford. You would have thought it easy to cross reference the lists in the Parish Magazine with the Census; after all, it is only a three year gap; but not a bit of it. I have found some of the volunteers in the Census lists, but less than half. In several cases, the census gives surnames which are the same as the volunteers and the right sort of age profile, but not the person himself. For others there is no clue as to why the volunteer is considered a Twyfordian.

Some allowance must be made for Twyford people living in Colden Common (the census for which I have not seen) but I think the best answer is this. Many of the volunteers are young single men who have travelled for work out of the village. They will have been born in Twyford and grown up in the village and when it comes to volunteering, they do so from their family home. So of the men aged 18 to 38 recorded as being in Twyford in the 1911 census, the volunteers are below the 50% level. Even so, the sudden exodus of fit young men from useful local jobs must have left the most enormous hole in village activity at all levels.

What did these young men do and were they all single? Of the 17 I have cross referenced, seven were under 20 in 1914, three between 20 and 30, and seven between 30 and 39. 12 were single; 13 were stable boys or carters, farm workers, gardeners, and there was a house boy and a shop assistant. One was an architect.

What were their motives for joining up? For many years prior to the actual declaration of war, there had been general anti-German feeling, fuelled by the press, but it seems to have been more akin to what a football fan might say or do, rather than genuine bellicosity. There had been so little first-hand experience of war to temper enthusiasm; the Boer war had finished twelve years before; the Afghan wars were small scale frontier wars; both were a long, long way away and none had been on European soil. Neither were modern wars between two fully industrialised powers. How could they imagine what was to come? They thought that there would be a quick scrap, some bloody noses and then they would all be home, victorious, by Christmas.

There were, at the same time, particularly as the crisis grew, expressions of great reluctance to go to war, but with a great deal of self-righteousness. When finally war was declared, public opinion moved overwhelmingly behind the war with Germany and Austria, and doubts vanished. The King and Queen were cheered for three hours after his first wartime speech. At the beginning of August 1914, Parliament issued a call for an extra 100,000 soldiers; recruitment was high. However, the real recruiting boom began in the last week of August, when news of the British retreat following the Battle of Mons reached Britain. Recruiting peaked in the first week of September.

Financial considerations were not the primary motive; a trooper's wage was 1/- per day plus keep, whereas the agricultural workers wage (for a 58 hour week) was 16/9, plus a cottage. For married men, one powerful reassurance was the pension for themselves, if injured, or for their widow, if killed.

Then there was the motive of adventure; the army, the navy and the war provided entirely new horizons. You can imagine how a group of lads who had grown up together would encourage each other and how if one went, so would they all. Contrast this with the alternatives for an unskilled villager, - low pay, insecurity, hard labour, long hours and little hope of change.

Adventure was not the foremost thought, as Vera Brittain describes in the 'Testament of Youth' or Robert Graves in 'Goodbye to All That'. They and their privileged friends seem to have had a better appreciation of the potential horrors, but for all that, they saw joining up perhaps as duty, perhaps as destiny.

As we know, but they did not, they would not be home, victorious, by Christmas; many would not be home at all and those that did return would come back changed, often as strangers. And in the meantime the village had to live with the steady flow of bad news of their friends and relatives, from the first Twyford death in early September 1914 for a further four long years.

Chris Corcoran

Reference:

1. "Twyford: 20th Century Chronicles", ed Stanley Crooks, Geo Mann Publications, Nov 2000 - ISBN 0-95-244249-3.

2. TWYFORD'S WAR MEMORIAL

The village's First World War memorial was designed by St Mary's Church architect, George H Kitchin, and took the form of a carved oak screen into which were set five individual panels bearing the roll of honour. The panelling was designed to be placed on the west wall of the church and was moved later to its present position, facing east below the new balcony.

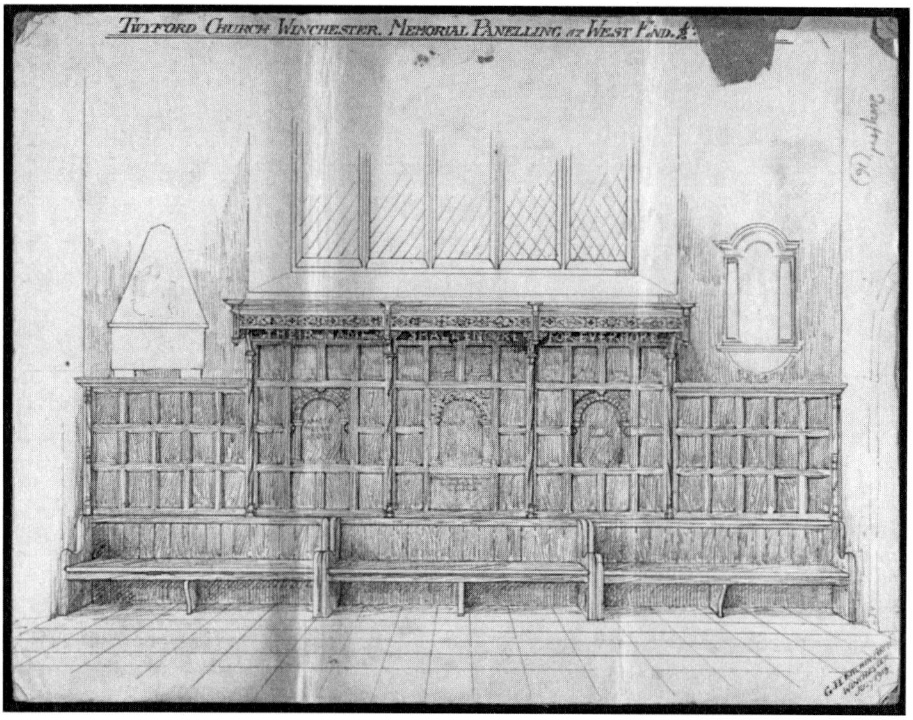

Original design of the memorial screen, by George H Kitchin

The Carved Panels on the Memorial Today

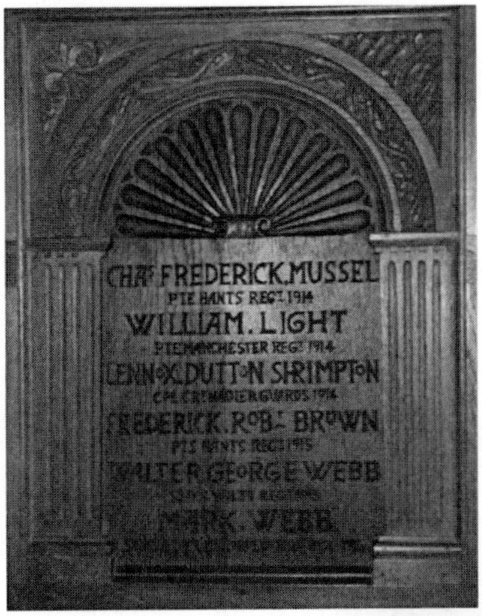

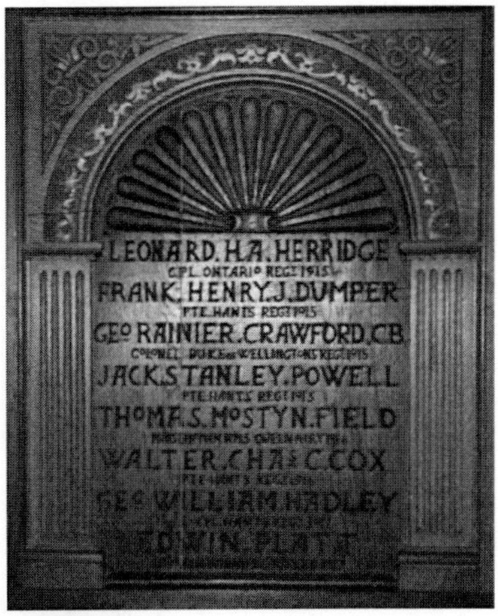

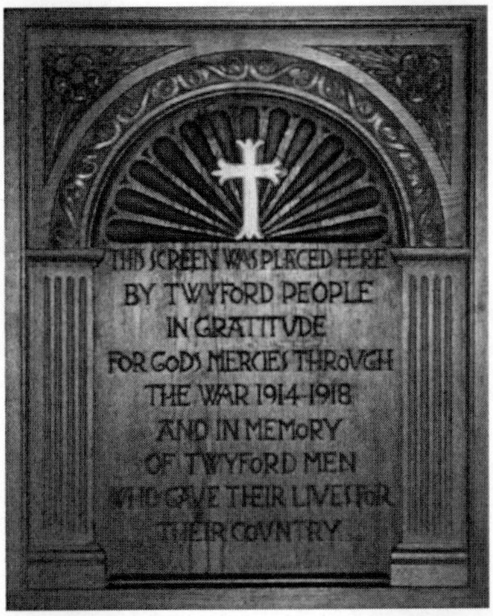

The panels show the full name, rank, regiment or ship and year of death of each man.

The design was drawn up in 1919 and authorisation of the Church authorities sought in March 1920. Across the top of the screen appears the legend "THEIR NAME LIVETH FOR EVERMORE" and the central panel reads:

> *This screen was placed here by Twyford people in gratitude for God's mercies through the war 1914-1918 and in memory of Twyford men who gave their lives for their country*

The Parish Magazines of January to April 1920 record the progress with the memorial. The first shows the names due to appear, the February edition lists the subscribers and contributors, many were parents of the lost men, in April it was installed and the last records dedication of the panels at the evening service on Sunday 18 April 1920.

Reference:

1. St Mary's PCC Faculty for installation of the War Memorial. Hampshire County Records Office, archive no. 21M65/404F/17.

3. THE MEN ON THE MEMORIAL

The Mussell Brothers, Chas Frederick and Sydney A

Private Charles Frederick Mussell Hampshire Regiment (January 1893 – 15 September 1914) and Sergeant Sydney Arthur Mussell Hampshire Regiment (1896 – 29 August 1918)

Charles Frederick and Sydney Arthur were brothers, the two sons of Frederick William and Frances Amelia Mussell of Queen Street, Twyford.

Tracing the family back to the 18th century, the boys' great-grandfather, John Mussell was born c1791 in West Grimstead, a small village five miles SE of Salisbury. By 1831 it had a population of only 186. He married Jane Hayter, a fellow villager, in the 12th century village church, St John's, on 22 August 1822. The 1838 Tithe Map shows John as the owner of the land he farmed at Popes Bottom and as the tenant of other land owned by the Earl of Radnor, the major landowner in the village. John died on 4 April 1878 and was buried in the village churchyard.

John and Jane had at least nine children. Charles was the eldest son. He was baptised on 10 October 1822 at St John's and married Elizabeth Humby on 26 November 1846 in St Thomas Church, Salisbury. He seems to have had some schooling, presumably in the village, for by 1851 he was a schoolmaster in Alderbury and by 1861 the master of the Workhouse in Amesbury. There he would have been expected to teach. At some point prior to 1871 the family had moved to Wharf Road, Milland, Winchester. The 1871 census shows him there with Elizabeth and a growing family of four. He prospered. By 1881 the family had moved to 21 Bar End and he was describing himself as "dairyman of 14 acres and employing six men". Charles died on the 26 June 1884 at Bar End, and left a personal estate of £547, a not inconsiderable sum for that date.

Frederick William, the son of Charles and Elizabeth, was born in Salisbury but baptised at St Maurice's Church, Winchester, on 10 August 1862. He helped his father, and then his widowed mother, in the dairy business. He married in 1890 and he and his wife, Frances Amelia, had seven children, two of whom died young. They moved to a five-roomed house in Queen Street, Twyford c1900 from where Frederick William worked as a cattleman and then as a water keeper.

Two sons survived to manhood. Charles Frederick was born in Winchester in 1893,

Sydney Arthur in Eastleigh in 1896. In 1911, still living in Queen Street, Charles Frederick was employed as a school porter and Sydney Arthur as a domestic house boy.

Charles Frederick Mussell

He had a short war and was the village's first casualty. He was reported in the September 1914 Parish Magazine as having enlisted in the Hampshire Regiment, one of five young men from the village. He had been one of the members of the Church Lads' Brigade Company who enlisted during the summer of 1914.

His unit was the 1st Battalion, Hampshires, which was in Colchester when war broke out. The regiment was held back from the original British Expeditionary Force by a last minute decision to defend England against a possible German invasion. The fate of the BEF in France and the lack of any move by the Germans to invade reversed that decision and the 1st Hampshires moved to Harrow to prepare for France. They left for Southampton on 22 August, from where they sailed to Le Havre. The troops were moved up to the front, to Solesmes, almost immediately. For the next ten days they manoeuvred in the area to the east of Cambrai, Amiens, Compiegne & Soissons, occasionally engaging the enemy but mostly retreating towards Paris. By early September, however, it was the Germans who were in retreat. The campaign was still one of cavalry activity and continuous movement. Conditions for the troops were unpleasant, with very little rest, bad weather, some heavy fighting and few comforts – the diary of Private Pattenden reports on 3 September that *"I had a great treat today; a bathe in the moat of the chateau where we camp. It is the first time I have been fully undressed since 9 August"*. On 25 August the Regimental Diary records nine killed, 131 wounded and 42 missing, out of a complement of less than 1,000.

By 14 September the battalion was entrenched at La Montaigne Ferme, in a village called Lucy le Long, a few miles east of Soissons, on a hillside overlooking a long valley. They came under heavy German artillery fire from a battery some 1,500 yards to the front. There were 11 British deaths, all from artillery fire, and amongst them was Charles Frederick.

The November Parish Magazine reported his death:-

> *"We record with deep regret the first loss in the men of Twyford in this war of 1914. Charles Frederick Mussell died of wounds on September 15, at the age of 21 years. It was but the other day that he was one of our Church Lads' Brigade Company, then he joined the Hampshire Regiment. Now a greater call has*

come, and his name is on that roll of honour which every nation keeps of her sons who have given their lives in the defence of their country."

He was awarded, posthumously, three medals – the 1914 Star for active service in France up to 22 November 1914; the Victory Medal which was awarded to all who received, inter alia, the 1914 Star; and the British War Medal which was awarded to all who served.

He has no known grave and is commemorated on the memorial at La Ferte-Sous-Jouarre, Seine et Marne, Stone no 16.

Sydney Arthur Mussell

The 2/4 Battalion Hampshire Regiment was formed in September 1914 on Salisbury Plain as a home service unit. It sailed for India on 13 December and remained there until April 1917. By early 1915 six recruits from Twyford – all from the village's Bible Class – had joined the regiment and were quartered in Kitchener's Barracks in Quetta, a large strategic city on the North West Frontier in what is now Pakistan. Although far from the main action in Europe, the normal safeguarding of the Empire's frontiers continued. A 1915 letter from Frank Dumper, quoted on page 37, describes a patrol and other aspects of their life on the frontier that Sydney would have shared, together with the fact that, with the other Twyford men, he had joined the Royal Army Temperance Association.

By August 1916 Sydney Arthur had been promoted to lance corporal.

The Egyptian Expeditionary Force (EEF) was formed in March 1916, initially to protect the Suez Canal, but after Gallipoli it swiftly grew into a large reserve force designed to provide reinforcements for the Western Front and to engage in more offensive actions against the Ottoman Turks. It was composed mostly of Empire and British troops. The 2/4 Hampshire Battalion sailed from India on 29 April 1917 bound for Suez to join this force. On 30 May 1917 the battalion finally arrived at Zeitun, a district of Cairo. Until the middle of September the troops trained and acclimatised themselves in Sinai. Only on 13 September did the battalion come under fire.

After initial victories, the EEF suffered two defeats in attempts to capture Gaza in Southern Palestine. This led to stalemate in this theatre for six months from April 1917. In October the EEF advanced on Jerusalem and the Hampshire battalion, as part of the 75th Division, was heavily involved in the seven-day Battle of Nebi Samwil, which was the first attempt to capture the city. Nebi Samwil was on a hill from which the army could see into Jerusalem some five miles distant. When the British launched their next offensive early in December, the city fell surprisingly easily.

The Hampshire losses at the battle were 14 killed, 86 wounded and five missing. This was fighting of the kind that had not been seen in India.

Following serious losses on the Western Front during the German spring offensive in March 1918, reinforcements from the EEF were sent to Europe. At the end of April the battalion embarked for France arriving at Marseille on 1 June. They were attached to the 62nd West Riding Brigade and took part in the 2nd Battle of the Marne. In ten days heavy fighting in July in the Ardre valley there were 353 casualties, killed, wounded or missing. The battalion was withdrawn from the battle until the 29 August when, in what their commanding officer called a "little action", five men were killed, among them Acting Sergeant Mussell, then in 'A' Company. It seems likely that he was killed by friendly artillery fire. The battalion's diary reads "Artillery fire had been asked for which inflicted further casualties on the enemy but unfortunately one or two short shells killed one or two of our own men."

He was awarded two medals, the Victory and the British War. He was twenty-two. He is buried in the Mory Abbey Military Cemetery, Mory in the Pas de Calais, the grave reference is V. A. 23.

Frederick William and Frances Amelia lived until after the Second World War. Their deaths were registered in Ware, Hertfordshire, his in 1952 and hers in 1947. Frances Amelia had been born in Stanstead. For whatever reason, it seems they had returned to live where her roots were.

Colin Oram.

Editor's Note

1. Church Lads' Brigade. An Anglican youth organisation with branches in the UK and overseas. Formed in 1891, the Church Lads' Brigade with its sister organisation, the Church Nursing and Ambulance Brigade for Young Women and Girls, later the Church Girls' Brigade, are still active.

Lennox Dutton Shrimpton

Corporal Lennox Dutton Shrimpton Grenadier Guards (27 September 1893 – 5 November 1914)

Lennox Dutton Shrimpton was born on 27 September 1893 in Nottingham, the son of Alexander James Shrimpton (1863-1908) from Hampshire and Kate Elizabeth Kaines (1866-1955) of Twyford.

Lennox's mother was one of eight children, born and brought up in Twyford, the daughter of a butcher/dealer, living at Water Farm in 1871. His father Alexander Shrimpton, one of seven children, was also from Hampshire, living in Twyford for a time when he was very young. He married Kate in Winchester in 1892. Later they moved to Nottingham to work in the clothing and textile industry. They lived at 38 Burford Road, it was a middle class area of the city.

Lennox was the eldest of three children. He had two sisters, Winifred who had died in 1900 aged only two and Edith born in 1902.

Tragically in 1908 Lennox's father died aged just 44, at St Leonard's on Sea in Sussex, a place frequented by the family. Lennox was 16 at the time and his sister Edith only six. He was a pupil at the High Pavement Grammar School in Stanley Road, just a short walk from their home in Nottingham.

He took the School Certificate Examination, the predecessor to 'O' Levels, in 1908/09, and passed, with a 3rd Class mark. We have no record as to whether he stayed on after 16/17, but a couple of years later, in 1911, he was living at 11 Cranmer Grove with his mother and sister and was working as a Drapers Assistant. Bear in mind that since the 17th century Nottingham had been the centre of the English hosiery and later in the 19th century the lace-making industries.

However drapery was not to be Lennox's calling. Later in 1911, in June, when he was 18, he joined the Regular Army. He signed on in Nottingham on the 27th and committed to a 'Short Service' contract, which meant three years' service with the Colours followed by a further nine with the Reserves. He joined the Grenadier Guards and three days later, on the 30th, was at the Guards Depot at Caterham where he was assigned to the 1st Battalion; his regimental number was 15313. Because the Guards regiments' records were kept separately from those of the rest of the army, more of them survived the Second World War bombing that destroyed those of many of the other men on our memorial. Those for Lennox paint a picture for us of this 17 year 9 month-old young man. He was 5 feet 8¾ inches tall with a fresh complexion, brown hair and blue eyes, and fit, weighing in at 125 lbs, 8 stone 13 lbs.

His service was likely to have been in London. Nervous of labour unrest, the government retained a military presence in the capital, and Lennox would have been involved in ceremonial and guard duties as well. Things must have gone pretty well for him, on 19 September 1912 he was promoted to lance corporal. But was there a hiccup? On the 17 January 1913 there is a cryptic comment in his record "Disc ? LCpl Pt" and all subsequent references to him are as a Private or, later, Guardsman.

Ah well, in any event the end of his three years' service came the following year, on 27 June 1914. He was paid off and transferred to the Reserves, his papers describing him as "A very clean smart man". Interestingly army life clearly did something for Lennox. Was it a good diet and regular exercise that accounted for growth of an inch and a quarter, his discharge papers record him as 5 feet 10 inches tall.

We have no record of where Lennox spent the next five weeks. It's not clear whether his mother had moved to Twyford by then. Anyway it must have been a disturbing time. War fever gripped the country and, for a 20-year-old, Lennox may have left his mates with some misgivings ... However it was to be only until the 5th August, when he was called back to the Colours in the general mobilisation. He had been away from the regiment for just 39 days.

On return he was assigned to the 2nd Battalion which was being brought up to war strength – 30 officers and 1,100 other ranks. A very few days later they left for France, travelling on the SS Cawdor Castle (6,243 tons) which arrived in Le Havre on 13 August. The battalion was ecstatically welcomed in the port and made its way by train to Rouen and then Amiens. The regimental historian, Frederick Ponsonby[1], records "Fervent scenes of welcome went on all along the line. Each little wayside station, every bridge and level crossing held a cheering throng." (page 16.) More slowly now the train went on through Cambrai, Busigny, Vaux Andigny to Flavigny, where they detrained. This was on 15 August. On the 20th they heard guns for the first time. Further marching and countermarching. They fired their weapons in anger on 24 August. What followed was the Retreat from Mons with its endless marching and fighting.

Thereafter the battalion took part in the Battle of the Marne, 5 - 12 September, then almost immediately into the Battle of the Passage of the Aisne, up to early October. All of this involved almost endless movement and countermovement as the armies jockeyed for position, with the Germans exploiting their general superiority in numbers. At practically every stop the men had to entrench to protect against artillery fire and the rapid movements of the enemy. But these were real battles and the battalion sustained heavy losses. Ponsonby writes of the Passage of the Aisne, at one point, "A terrific explosion followed, and out of the 103 men who had been brought up, only 44 were left, all the rest being killed or wounded." (Page 70).

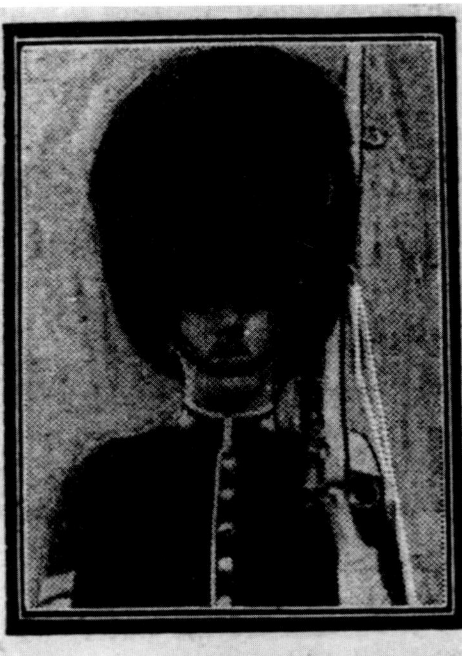

Corporal Lennox Dutton Shrimpton, Grenadier Guards, 12 Ivy Grove, Sherwood Rise, aged 21, died of wounds received near Ypres.

PTE. L. SHRIMPTON, Grenadier Guards. Killed in the first Battle of Ypres. Nephew of Mr. and Mrs. Whitear, 1, The Lees, Milward-crescent, Hastings.

In mid-October the battalion was moved, with the British Army, some 100 km north-west, reaching Hazebrouck on the 14th, 30 km south-west of Ypres. This was a part of Sir John French's plan for the British to be positioned to the left of the French, to enable more effective communication and supply from England, although the manoeuvre embraced the so-called 'Race to the Sea' as the German and Franco-British armies repeatedly attempted to outflank their opponents to their north.

As that move spluttered to a halt the protagonists found themselves drawn into the first of the Battles of Ypres, from 19 October to 22 November.

Ponsonby gives graphic descriptions of that time, a selection of quotes giving an idea of the nature of the battle and essentially of Lennox's last week ...

- *"The trenches, composed of isolated holes which held two or three men apiece, were exposed from the left to enfilade fire, but there the Battalion had to remain for two days shelled intermittently. (Ponsonby page 146)*
- *After a long wet night in the trenches, the 2nd Grenadiers were to have a still longer day's fighting – a day, too, in which they were "holding on by their eyelids. (page 154)*
- *On/about the 1st November, their Brigadier, Lord Cavan, sent the following message "The situation is extremely critical. You are to hold your ground at all costs. Sir Douglas Haig relies on the Grenadiers to save the First Corps and possibly the Army." (page 155)*
- *They were subjected to a furious and intense artillery bombardment. That night, by the light of a blazing farm in the middle of their front, the grenadiers "saw a spectacle, which later on grew more and more familiar. What had once been a field was now a mass of trenches; the whole place had been ploughed up by shells and the hedges were all torn up and burnt and blown to bits." (page 158)*
- *Battalion ordered into the wood south-east of the Brown Road to clear it with fixed bayonets, although found to be clear of Germans, and then ordered to dig in with very limited vision and fields of fire (page 160)*
- *Nov 2nd 4 vigorous attacks by the Germans. (page 162) "24 Killed, 12 Wounded, 1 Missing" (War Diary). That evening a special order was circulated by the C-in-C congratulating all and urging everyone to hold on (page 164)*
- *Nov 3rd spent in strengthening the trenches and in artillery exchanges*
- *"4th November. Same positions. Very heavy shelling most of the day. No real infantry attack, but enemy entrenching about 300 yards away. Very wet. 1st Line transport shelled and moved back through YPRES to farm near DICKEBUSCH. 4 Killed. 26 Wounded." (War Diary)*
- *By the 5th it began to be thought in the firing line that the enemy had abandoned all attempt to break through the line, but in reality he was waiting only for reinforcements ... was now determined to throw the whole weight of his superior numbers on Ypres. (page 165)*
- *5th November: "Remained in trenches at KLEIN ZILLEBEKE. Shelled most of the day and continually sniped. 3 Killed 5 Wounded." (War Diary)*
- *Furious fighting on 6th. No 1 Company practically wiped out." (page 168).*

The 5th is the date we have for Lennox's death from wounds received. One source says he died from wounds received in action on the 5th, another that he was killed on that day, another that he was killed on the 3rd. Either way he was a casualty of this deadly battle in which "The 2nd Battalion had been fighting incessantly from 21 October to 16 November." (page 180).

Regarding this same period, General David Fraser writes of the battalion:

> *"On 11th November only 3 officers and 74 men were left. There had never before been comparable levels of casualties."* [2]

By the end of 1914 the old British regular Army had suffered massive casualties and lost most of its fighting strength. It had however managed to help stop the German advance. As a trained soldier and reservist Lennox had been part of this. Kaiser Bill had been famously dismissive of the British Expeditionary Force, allegedly issuing an order on 19 August to "... walk over General French's contemptible little army". Although he probably never heard the expression, had he lived Lennox would have been proud to have been one of "The Contemptibles".

After his death Lennox's mother returned to Hampshire, remarrying in 1916 Charles Raymond Read. They lived in Hornby Cottage (now Granary Cottage) in Queen Street, Twyford. Sadly he died two years later in 1918. When Kate died in 1955 aged 89, she was living on the Otterbourne Road, in a house called 'Lennox', which is still there today. Although Lennox was born and raised in Nottingham, his family roots were very much in Twyford. His Great Grandparents Benjamin and Harriett Vokes (nee Latham) had run The Volunteer public house in Queen Street for many years.

Melancholy notes from Lennox's army file ... the 'Register of Soldiers Effects' shows the sum of one shilling in Lennox's account, authorised for disbursement to 'Kate. E. Read' in August 1920. And an air of finality is conveyed by a War Office calculation in his personal file, his Military History Sheet, computed three years and 55 days of Home service before posting to the Reserves, and 77 days following Call-Up in 1914, making a total of four years and 132 days of military service, or almost 20% of this young man's life, when he died, aged 21.

He is buried in the Perth Cemetery (China Wall) in Belgium, West Vlaanderen, plot ref. 111.h.20. It was called Perth (as the predecessors of the 2nd Scottish Rifles were raised in Perth), and China Wall after the communication trench in the area known as the Great Wall of China, or sometimes as the Halfway House Cemetery.

Lennox is not only remembered on our war memorial in St Mary's Church, Twyford. His name also appears on the High Pavement School war memorial and was on the memorial in St Augustine's Church, New Basford, Nottingham. This was later demolished and its memorial was transferred to St Leodegarius Church, in Old Basford.

The Medal Roll shows Lennox's decorations to have included the 1914 Star, the Victory Medal and the British War Medal.

Vanessa Croucher

References:

1. The Grenadier Guards in the Great War of 1914-1918, Lieut. Colonel The Right Hon. Sir Frederick Ponsonby (Late Grenadier Guards) 1920 Macmillan and Co. Limited, St Martin's Street, London.
2. The Grenadier Guards, General Sir David Fraser, Pub 1978, Osprey Publishing Ltd ISBN 0 85045 284 8.
3. War Diary, 2nd Battalion, The Grenadier Guards August – December 1914. National Archives WO 95/1342/1 Sheet 25.

William Light

Private William Light Manchester Regiment (1889 - 11 December 1914)

William Light's exact date of birth is uncertain but was probably in 1889 in the Parish of Trinity, Winchester. Documentation of his Twyford connection begins in the 1901 England Census when he is described as being 12 years old and living, with his brother Robert then aged ten, as "Boarders" in the household of Mr John Maton and his wife Mary J. Maton in Seagers (sic) Lane in the Civil Parish of Twyford. Intriguingly the 1911 England Census records one "Mrs. Light" as the lone female in a household with two males (possibly William and Robert) living at "The Old House at Home" Public House in the Ecclesiastical Parish of Holy Trinity Colden Common, and the Civil Parish of Twyford Hampshire.

William Light enlisted in the First Battalion Manchester Regiment in Winchester as a private, his number was 1907. The Regiment was stationed in Lahore and Karachi (now Pakistan) at the outbreak of war, and reached Marseille on 26 September 1914. William Light died ten weeks later. His story is one of many similar ones but points us directly at the appalling scale of the countless tragedies of the First World War.

The 1st Battalion Manchester Regiment fought at the Battle of La Bassee (Canal), First Battle of Messines, and the Battle of Armentieres on the Western Front in 1914. This Front, in the region of Ypres and the river Lys saw action throughout the 51 months of the First World War. It was described as "complete" by the end of the battles for La Bassee canal on 18 October 1914, which also marked what historians call the end of the "war of movement" (into the fixed positions of the opposing armies). Movement only really began again in the last few months of 1918 leading up to Allied victory. In between was the "war of position", starting with the First Battle of Ypres fought between 19 October and 22 November 1914.

Perhaps the "war of position" should have been called the "war of attrition" in hindsight; I quote Yves le Maner, Director of La Coupole History and Remembrance Centre in Northern France:

> *"In the winter that followed (1914/1915) the sector of the (river) Lys became a "forgotten front" where soldiers suffered in the badly organised trenches, with mediocre supplies. The threat of death hung over them from the bullets of expert marksmen, unexpected mines, heavy shelling, and the murderous attacks they were ordered to carry out on the lines of the enemy."*

William Light's war record tells us he was killed in action in the Western European Theatre on 11 December 1914. His battalion and regiment were not then engaged in a named battle, but in this war of position. He has no known grave or grave stone, but is named, along with 13,000 other Officers and Men who had fallen by 25 September 1915 and whose bodies were never recovered, on the War Graves Memorial at Le Touret Military Cemetery, Richebourg, Nord-Pays-de-Calais, near where he served and died. His Medal Card is shown below.

If he had seen action for ten weeks, that was less than one twentieth (5%) of the 1,566 days of the First World War, but he had become one of 8,528,831 known deaths on both sides and one of 13,770 deaths from his Regiment alone. William Light's short story might well have been that of the Unknown Soldier to whom we owe so much.

Andrew Brooks.

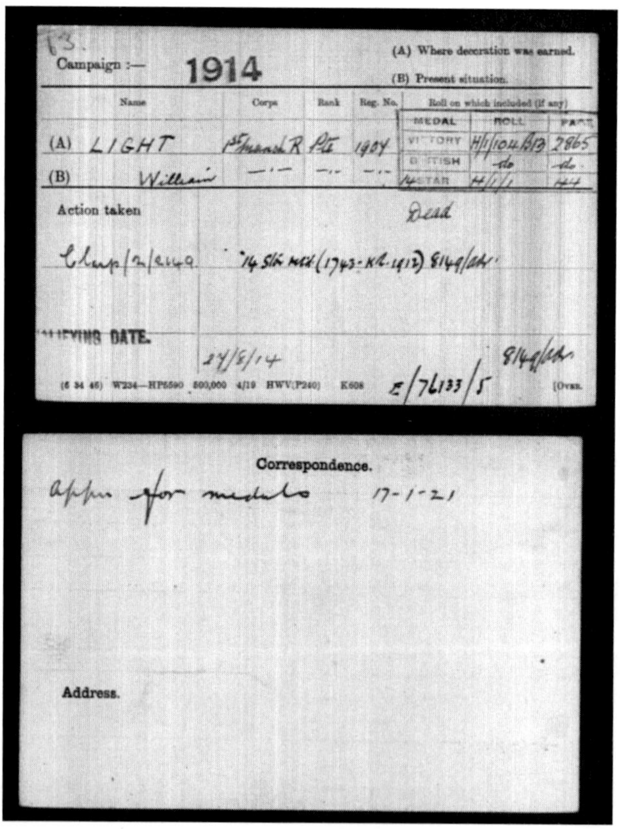
Campaign :— 1914

(A) Where decoration was earned.
(B) Present situation.

Name	Corps	Rank	Reg. No.	Medal	Roll	Page
(A) LIGHT	1st Manch R	Pte	1904	VICTORY	H/1/104 B13	2865
(B) William	—	—	—	BRITISH	do	do
				14 STAR	H/1/1	44

Action taken: Dead

Correspondence.

Appln for medals 17-1-21

Address.

William Light's Medal Card

Frederick Robt Brown

Private Frederick Robert Brown Hampshire Regiment (28 December 1898 – 26 April 1915)

In 1922 the Battles Nomenclature Committee of the War Office published its final report, *"The official names of the battles and other engagements fought by the military forces of the British Empire during the Great War 1914-1919 and the Third Afghan War 1919"*. At this distance it's tempting to think that the great battles with which we are now so familiar, Ypres, The Somme, Passchendaele, etc. were ever known thus, that they had tidy beginnings and discrete ends. Of course the reality was quite different. Diaries written at the time describe a much lower level of detail and local features predominate in the participants' descriptions of the struggles. Between the 22 April and 25 May 1915, there were four consecutive battles around the Ypres Salient[1], the Battles of Gravenstafel Ridge, St. Julien, Frezenberg Ridge and Bellewaerde Ridge. The Nomenclature Committee 'tidied these up' into the Second Battle of Ypres.

In October 1914 the Germans had actually occupied Ypres, a significant transport hub and commercial centre in Flanders. But by dint of concerted allied effort (the First Battle of Ypres), they were thrown back some 8-10 km to form the Salient, with the German Front Line re-established on slightly higher ground to the north, east and south of the town.

And so the scene was set for the Second Battle of Ypres six months later. This was notorious for being the first use of gas on the Western Front, on the 22 April at the Battle of Gravenstafel Ridge. The Germans had tried it, unsuccessfully, on the Russian front, where it froze and failed to deploy effectively. However its use at Ypres was to have deadly impact and to influence operations on the Western Front for the rest of the war, and of course subsequently.

However there were warnings that the allies failed to pick up. On 28 March a British raid on the German trenches at Zillebeke, south-east of Ypres, resulted in the capture of a German officer. In good English he wrote a statement to the effect that gas cylinders had been installed in no-man's-land and that when the wind was favourable the gas was to be released towards the British trenches. To verify this the British sent out a patrol to investigate. They found dozens of cylinders just as the German officer had described. The information was passed on to British headquarters but the event was not mentioned again until one of the men in the patrol wrote a letter to the Daily Express, 18 years later.[2]

And a fortnight later, on Tuesday 13 April, a second warning came when a German soldier, Private August Jaeger, climbed out of his front-line trench and scrambled across the few hundred metres of no-man's-land to desert to the French. During his subsequent interrogation Jaeger readily gave details about German troop strength, routines and gun batteries and he revealed plans for the imminent use of gas:-

> *"An attack is planned for the near future against the French trenches of the above mentioned sector. With this object in view four batteries have been placed in position in the first line trenches ...; these batteries each have 20 bottles of asphyxiating gas. Each company has 4 such batteries. Each battery has 5 gunners. At a given signal - 3 red rockets fired by the artillery - the bottles are uncorked, and the gas on escaping, is carried by a favourable wind towards the French trenches. This gas is intended to asphyxiate the men who occupy the trenches and to allow the Germans to occupy them without losses. In order to prevent the men being themselves intoxicated by the gas, each man is provided with a packet of tow[3] steeped in oxygen."* [4]

Despite the dissemination of this warning, when the release of gas came on 22 April the impact was devastating. The French troops who were the immediate target abandoned their trenches and fled in panic to avoid the deadly greenish-yellow cloud. The result was that a five kilometre gap opened up in the Allied line with gassed stragglers from the front line wandering in a state of acute shock 3-4 km behind their positions. Although the Germans failed fully to exploit this opportunity, their troops had advanced 4-5 km into the salient and a very substantial breakthrough was in prospect.

Later in the afternoon of the 22 April the 1st Battalion Hampshire Regiment, part of the 11th Brigade, was billeted in farms about 2 km from BAILLEUL and some 20 km from Ypres. They were warned to get ready to move at short notice.

On 24 April they left BAILLEUL by train and that afternoon and the following day marched towards the sound of the guns.

The Battalion War Diary for the period is pretty brief, but includes a gripping description written by the battalion Commanding Officer after the events. Here are some relevant excerpts:

> *"The Hampshires were leading the Brigade. It was a horrid situation, there was a great gap, we were to fill it and nobody knew where our ends of the gap were or where were the enemy.*
>
> *At 2.25 am on the 26th we reached the top of a slight ridge: we knew we must be near the Royal Fusiliers and there was only an hour of darkness left. There*

was no time to lose and we started to dig. The men were tired out. They dug like bricks. Most of them knew that their lives depended on their being underground by dawn. ... the morning was misty, so we were able to go on digging for another couple of hours which made all the difference.

With the lifting of the mist (at 7.00 am on the 26th) the German guns opened. It is hopeless to attempt to describe it. Owing to our being at the extreme point of the salient we had guns almost all round us ... For 8 days and nights their guns never ceased. At times shells were falling on our trenches at the rate of about 50 a minute.

The 26th was our worst day ... Over 100 casualties occurred this day."[5]

One of this 100 was Private Frederick Robert Brown, number 3/4050, of Twyford. He had joined up in 1914 and spent the remainder of that year and early 1915 undergoing basic training in the Winchester area. In late March 1915 he was sent to join the Regiment at Ploegsteert, in one of the drafts making good the regiment's losses of the previous year.

Before joining up however Frederick had attended to a significant matter of personal business. He changed his name. He had been born 'Kinder' and perhaps he anticipated anti-German feeling making life difficult for him in the army. By 1911 his mother had remarried and he was living as part of the Brown family, with his sister Alice Adeline, and two half-sisters, Edith Emily Brown and Dorothy May Brown, who were eight and three years old respectively. He was not alone in changing his name as, of course, some two years later the Royal Family came to a similar conclusion and changed their family name to 'Windsor'.

But, stepping further back, Frederick Robert Kinder was born in Eastleigh, in 1898. He was born at home at 9 Factory Road[6], near to the railway wagon works where his father Arthur worked as a labourer. He and Frederick's mother, Edith Margaret, nee Cutler from Wimborne in Dorset, had married in 1897 in Christchurch where she had been working as a general servant. Frederick's sister Alice was born on 2 February 1900. Sadly after only three years of marriage Arthur, who had signed up to fight in the Boer War, died on a troopship bound for South Africa, on 24 June 1900. He had been a bandsman in The Kings Royal Rifle Corps.

So in 1901 we have a record of the reduced family, still living at their home in Factory Road, Eastleigh. The widowed Edith was only 27, Frederick was two years old and Alice one.

However only a year later their fortunes were looking up, Edith had married again. Her new husband was James Brown (born 1881) and they married in 1902 in the Winchester area. They had two daughters, Edith born in Hythe and Dorothy born in Sway. By 1911 the family was living in Spring Lane Colden Common with James running his own business as a master butcher. The household included Frederick's mother, his sister and two half-sisters and William Rose, 21, who worked for James as a Butcher's Roundsman. Frederick's age is recorded as 15 at this time and he 'assists at home', by which I guess they meant helped to run the shop.

Finally we need to consider the subject of Frederick's age. Three documents guide us on this, his Birth Certificate and the two census records. These latter say that he was two in April 1901 and 15 in 1911. The former is correct but the latter some three years out. Was Edith genuinely confused when she made the return in 1911, perhaps Frederick really was a big boy or should he have been at school rather than 'helping at home'. Either way it certainly looks as though Frederick was only 15 when he joined up and 16 when he left the country the following year, and of course only 16 when he was killed. Certainly his later family were well aware that he was an underage soldier, his great nephew Clive Copestake reports his grandmother telling him in hushed, conspiratorial tones that "Frederick had put his age up to join the Army".

The sad afterword for this sixteen-year-old was that on 25 October 1919 Edith Margaret received the grand sum of two pounds, eighteen shillings and tuppence as a war gratuity and a little later Frederick's medals, the 1914/15 Star, the War medal and the Victory medal. He has no known grave and is remembered on the Menin Gate in Ypres, Index No M.R. 29, Part XIV.

Vanessa Croucher
Christopher Pope

Notes:

1. Salient. A jutting out or prominent part of a system of fortifications or trenches, an outward bulge in a line of military attack or defence. At Ypres the salient was about 10 km wide at its base and projected 8 km into German-held territory.
2. Gas! The Battle for Ypres 1915, p. 18 (acknowledgement to Major General C H Foulkes, Gas! The Story of the Special Brigade, Edinburgh, Blackwood & Sons Ltd., 1934) [http://www.greatwar.co.uk/battles/second-ypres-1915/prelude/cylinders-discovered.htm].

3. Tow. A bundle of loose fibres, probably cotton or flax, formed into a pad, which, when impregnated with suitable chemicals and held over the face, was the initial response for providing protection against gas attack.
4. Official History of the Canadian Forces in The Great War 1914-1919, Volume I, Chronology, Appendices and Maps, Appendix no. 320, p. 228-229 [http://www.greatwar.co.uk/battles/second-ypres-1915/prelude/deserter-jaeger.htm]
5. War Diary, 1st Battalion Hampshire Regiment, Ref. WO-95-1495-0-475, attachment at page 86 by Lieut. Colonel F.R. Hicks, "Move from Ploegsteert to Ypres".
6. 9 Factory Road. Although Factory Road still exists, the lower order numbers have been lost as part of the Swan Centre and new Wells Place development. No 9 could almost be the McDonalds there today!

Leonard H A Herridge

Corporal Leonard Henry Ross Herridge Ontario Regiment (29 August 1893 - 15 June 1915)

Leonard Herage was Twyford born and bred and lived in the village until he went to Canada in 1911. He was born on 29 August 1893 and baptised at St Mary's Church Twyford on 1 October: Leonard Henry Ross Herage, the son of Fanny Louisa Herage a single woman. His father's name is not recorded. The 1901 census finds him, then aged seven, living with his grandparents, James and Louisa Herage in Park Lane Twyford. James was then a platelayer on the railway, aged 61 and born in Hartley Row Hampshire. Louisa 59 was born in Twyford. James, the son of Joseph Herage, married Louisa Young aged 18 in Twyford Church on 15 June 1861: they were to have a large family.

James Herage

Meanwhile Leonard's mother Fanny had got married, to John Dyke on 3 January 1898 at Twyford, he was a private soldier in the Hampshire Regiment. In 1901 they too were in Park Lane, only two doors up from James, Louisa and Leonard, with two children, sons aged two and six months. By 1911 they had moved to 48 High Street Eastleigh and had six children: John was a postman.

In 1911 Leonard, then 17, was working as a shepherd and still living with his grandparents. But soon after the census in that year he moved to Canada, leaving Liverpool on 29 April 1911 on SS Canada, destination port Quebec. He was to join his uncle Herbert, his mother's younger brother who had emigrated to Canada earlier. (Family information suggests he met his wife Eveline on the ship). The 1911 Canadian census, taken on 9 June, finds Leonard in the household of Herbert Herage and his wife Eveline: they had a two-year-old daughter, Gladis, and were living in Walkerville, Ontario. Family information indicates Leonard went to work as a machinist in the Ford factory just over the border in Detroit. Canadian Border crossings show he arrived there in August 1911.

Leonard volunteered soon after the start of the war. His Attestation Papers are dated 31 August 1914 when he was passed fit for the Canadian Expeditionary Force. He is recorded as having served four years in the 21st Essex (Ontario) Fusiliers (there is some discrepancy here as he only arrived in Canada in May 1911). He gave his mother Mrs J Dyke as next of kin and signed the Declaration and Oath on 17 September 1914. He was 5ft 8ins tall with fair hair and blue eyes and had tattoos on both arms. He joined as a private and his regimental number was 6346.

The training camp to which volunteers were sent was at Valcartier, some 16 miles north of Quebec City. The first volunteers reached the camp on 18 August, but by 8 September there were over 30,000. Conditions at Valcartier were initially very sparse with few facilities, and the organising, equipping and training of the first contingent was a major undertaking.

The 21st Essex Fusiliers formed part of the 1st Battalion (Western Ontario) Regiment which was part of the 1st Brigade, 1st Canadian Division. Other records show the battalion referred to as 1st Battalion Canadian Infantry.

Leonard Herage was on the SS Laurentic which was one of 31 ships conveying the first contingent which left on 3 October 1914, escorted by four warships one bringing up the rear. After 12 days the convoy disembarked at Plymouth instead of Southampton, word having been given of German submarines in the English Channel. The disembarkation was described as an historic occasion, the arrival in Britain of the first large contingent of one of her overseas dominions. A few days later the contingent went by train first to Southampton, then proceeded to Salisbury Plain where they arrived to face bad weather after a sunny early autumn.

There were no permanent barracks for the Canadians and a programme of building huts began, into which most of the troops went, but the 1st Infantry Brigade remained throughout the winter in tents. The appalling weather conditions prevailed and to maintain morale all ranks were granted six days leave before Christmas with a free ticket to anywhere in the British Isles. It seems likely that Leonard went to Hampshire to visit his family, although his grandmother Louisa had died in October 1914. It would have been with some pride that the family learnt of Leonard's promotion to Lance Corporal on 31 December 1914, presumably shortly after he returned from leave. His grandfather, James Herage, would have learnt about this: he lived on until 1930, dying aged 91 'in the chair in the front room after his usual lunch time nap'.

After further training the main body of Canadian troops were inspected by King George V and Lord Kitchener. They sailed from Avonmouth in the West Country because of the continuing threat of submarines in the Channel. The troops were sent to the Front and inspected by Sir John French who commented very favourably on the Canadian contingent. During the second half of February 1915 the troops experienced some induction into trench warfare under guidance from British soldiers, before themselves going into the Front Line where the 1st Battalion faced its first test during the defence of St Julien, north of Ypres in late April and early May.

Leonard Herage

On 11 May 1915 Leonard Herage was promoted to corporal. The battalion was in action again at the Battle of Festubert. Thereafter it was in the line at Givenchy; for a period this was a relatively quiet section of the front.

Then, following a re-organisation of the British front by General Haig, an attack was planned primarily involving a British Corps immediately to the left of the Canadian position. A shortage of artillery ammunition led to a reduction in the scale of this attack, but the 1st Canadian Battalion was ordered to undertake an advance to protect and consolidate their flank with the British Corps. This element of the attack was on a very narrow, one-company, front. Careful preparation and extended artillery barrage could not entirely neutralise the opposing defenders. The position was complicated when British sappers exploded a mine designed to destroy an enemy strongpoint and the resulting debris caused casualties among the 1st Canadian Battalion. Each company of the battalion attacked in turn.[2] The success was very limited. Leonard Herage died in this attack, at what point is not recorded. His body was not recovered.

So Leonard was presumed to have died during the action at Givenchy and is commemorated on the Vimy Memorial, which is the memorial site in France dedicated to the memory of CEF forces killed in the First World War.

Leonard Herage was eligible and was posthumously awarded the 14-15 Star as Lance Corporal in the 1st Battalion, and the accompanying Plaque and Scroll (Serial No 757428) and the Memorial Cross; the latter is held by a member of the family, while the Plaque is in Roanoke, Virginia with Martin Rendle, Leonard's second cousin once removed. The Scroll is believed to be held by a Herage family member in Canada. The Scroll and Plaque were despatched in the early 1920s.

From 1 April 1915, when Leonard would have been in France, he assigned part of his pay to his mother Mrs Dyke, who was by then living in Chandlers Ford. Leonard's uncle, Herbert Herage enlisted in 1916: he survived the war and died in the 1940s.

Sue Kennedy.

References and Note

1. Service Record: Service File RG150, Accession 1992-93/166 Box 4285 - 2 Library and Archives of Canada
2. For a full description of the action at Givenchy on 15 June 1915 see G.W.L. Nicholson: Canadian Expeditionary Force 1914 – 1919, on line at www.cmp-cpm_forces.gc.ca/dhh/his/oh/index-eng.asp or 'Official History of the Canadian Army in the First World War: Canadian

Expeditionary Force, 1914-1919', Nicholson, G.W.L., pub: Duhamel, Queen's Printer and Controller of Stationery, Ottawa, 1964. Pages 104 and following.

3. There are members of the Herage family still living in the Twyford area, and a family member has traced the family, with various spellings, back to 1561 on the Hampshire/Berkshire borders.

Editor's Note

A word is necessary concerning Leonard's full name and its spelling. The section heading for each of these stories retains the form and spelling from Twyford's war memorial. As readers will have noticed in Leonard's case this differs significantly from the other form used more widely. In general the surname is found variously spelled between Herage and Herridge. In Leonard's case Herage is the spelling on the baptism register and in the 1901 census, on all the Canadian Military Records and on the Canadian VIMY Memorial. In 1911 grandfather James spelled it Heradge on the census form, but then he did manage to reduce his own age on the form from 63 in 1901 to 70 ten years later! When James came to be buried, in 1930, the parish register recorded him as Herridge. The Parish Hall boards show two Herages, H and L, and a 'W Herridge'. A general search of the parish registers confirms James' burial as the only Herridge, but there is a good dusting of Herages. Members of the family living in the area confirm this is how it is spelt, correspondence having been received from a family member supporting Herage. How Leonard became Herridge on our memorial we cannot explain, unless it is that the only informant was James and we have seen how reliable he could be. In Leonard's case a typo also seems to have crept onto the memorial regarding his third initial. He was clearly christened 'Ross' so the carved 'A' is most likely a mis-reading at some point of a hand-written 'R'.

Frank Henry J Dumper

Private Frank Henry James Dumper Hampshire Regiment (20 July 1895 – 2 July 1915)

When I walk to the end of our drive in Park Lane, turn right and make my way towards the junction with Love Lane, I arrive close to the spot where Henry and Annie Dumper welcomed their first-born son Frank Henry James, at Upper Little Bourne Lodge, on 20 July 1895. That same year Aston Villa had won the FA cup, The Importance of Being Earnest opened in London, The National Trust was founded and the British Army was engaged on the North West frontier. Henry Dumper, a domestic gardener married Annie (neé Herage) at St Mary's Church, Twyford, in 1892. Many Dumpers and Herages lived in Park Lane, formerly known as Stiffs Lane. The 1881 census has at least 16 from the two families. Before marrying, Annie with her sister Mabel worked as cook/servants at 27 Edgar Road in Winchester. I drove by last week to pick it out, still a handsome villa.

The Dumper's next child Fanny survived only a few weeks. Next came Margaret, then Herbert and finally Elsie in 1907, by which time they had moved to Queen Street and their Uncle Alfred lodged with them. In 1911 Uncle is still there but Frank now 15, has employment as a garden boy and is a member of the Church Lads' Brigade.

Two years later, in 1913, a landmark village institution came into being. Miss Leila Hull of Monks Barn began a Bible class for boys and Frank was amongst the 17 founder members. Twyford's young men were very proud to be Miss Hull's boys, in fact three present day villagers, David Eaton, Ian Wheeler and John Harfield all belonged. The group had a football team and Frank was captain. In spring 1914 the Parish magazine carried a report of an Easter Monday match in which he scored two goals.

Not just a sporty type, he and 12 other Bible class lads staged a play at the beginning of the year called "A Race to Dinner", to a packed Parish Hall audience. At the end of the evening, Frank, as captain, presented Mrs Mordant Shipley with a bouquet of carnations tied up with the club's green and white colours. Four of these young thespians would find themselves together again 12 months later in another place, another country and in different times. In December they enlisted and in that same Parish Hall a farewell supper was held for the fourteen young Twyford men leaving for India with the 2/4th Hampshire Regiment. "After a most excellent supper, a few kind words of advice were addressed to the lads by the Vicar and Colonel Yorke.

After games, the evening was brought to a close by the singing of a verse of the Brigade hymn and God Save the King".

The 4th Hants, based in Winchester, was a Territorial force for Home Service only, however it could volunteer for overseas service if necessary. Shortly after the outbreak of war, the battalion was split into 1/4th and 2/4th at Bustard Camp on Salisbury Plain. The War Office considered that as the Territorials were not trained to the level of the regulars, they could replace those on Garrison duty at the outposts of the Empire. The 1/4th sailed for India in October followed by 2/4th, Frank's Battalion; 30 Officers and 756 other ranks under the command of Lt Col W Naish. Their equipment had arrived only the day before departure and just 50% of the rifles issued could be fired with any safety! The SS Caledonia (torpedoed and sunk off Malta in 1916) slipped down the Solent on 13 December 1914. Onlookers who heard the far away roar of cheers could only conjecture that they were departing for the Front. Those with field glasses could see that this troopship was crowded with men in helmets – great sola topees! The journey lasted a month, the troops disembarking at Karachi on 11 January 1915.

Of the journey, Ernest Drew, also one of Miss Hull's boys, wrote:

> *"We had a pleasant journey across the Water but it was rather rough coming through the Bay of Biscay. We got to Port Said on Christmas Day"*

Another Hampshire soldier on the voyage recalls:

> *"Xmas Day was spent in Port Said and the Suez canal with two hours shore leave. The less said about turkey the better. It was a case of Turkey, Turkey everywhere but never a piece to eat and most of us spent a Happy Christmas on underdone mutton. Next morning we ran aground and for two hours nothing but desert on either side and turbulent Turks advancing to the attack. However, at 6am the Corporal of C Company fell out of bed and the resultant roll enabled the ship to free herself and continue her course."*

It seems the more likely resolution was recorded by a Sgt Bunch from Yateley:

> *"To get off, the troops had to go to the stern of the boat to raise the bows, Suez was reached at 10.30am. It looks a much cleaner town than Port Said. A railway runs near the canal between the towns. Indian troops are stationed at intervals. There are a few trenches. On the Egyptian bank there are several villages with irrigation systems. We are now anchored near Bombay. There is a large amount of shipping here and very large buildings.*

I hope shore leave will be allowed but there does not seem much chance. Our time is 5 hours earlier than England."

Imagine, many of these men may never have even left Hampshire. Ernest Drew wondered at the oxen drawing carts and all sorts of birds and coconuts growing. The ship docked in Karachi and the troops boarded the train for Quetta, northern India, now in Pakistan. An officer recorded the journey:

"Breakfast in the desert in the early morning was a fresh experience and the cool morning in a sun heated land a wonderful time, unequalled under western skies. Out came the 'dixies' and the company cooks were soon busy while the men lined up in their messes and were served with rations and mugs of strong char as we now learned to call it. Officers turned out in pyjamas or uniform to see the men fed. We were now travelling through Sind and after three days found ourselves running through red sandstone rocks, scarred and twisted into fantastic shapes and entered the Bolan Pass at a gradient so steep that two engines were barely sufficient to pull us. We gained the tableland, 5,000ft of altitude on which Quetta lies, and came within sight of our future home."

They arrived at Kitchener's Barracks, Quetta, at 12'oclock where they were met by no less than five bands, British and Indian. Suddenly planted in a foreign country, officers and men had to adapt themselves to new conditions and they showed themselves equal to the task. The first camp was at Chasma Tangi where training was chiefly in mountain warfare and Kitchener Techniques. By March they were further north in the Khyber Pass close to the Afghan border. By a wonderful stroke of luck, Frank wrote describing an exercise to Miss Hull and it was published in the parish magazine of May 1915.

"On Tuesday 2 March, we had a long route march of 18 miles. We started out at 9 o'clock in the evening and went nearly 9 miles up the Khyber Pass where we did some skirmishing for about an hour. After a little rest we started on the return march home by a different road; we had not marched more than three miles when we came to a stream with no bridge, so the only thing to be done was to wade through it, which was very refreshing to our legs. We reached barracks at about 4.30 and the first thing we did after being dismissed was to have our dinner, which was well deserved after walking 18 miles in the boiling hot sun and sand and dust almost up to our knees. I never thought I should go into the Khyber Pass, where Dad once

passed through as an escort to the late Lord Roberts. It is a pretty pass, the mountains are very steep and rugged."

He also mentions that all the old Bible Class members have joined the Royal Army Temperance Association and that letters from Twyford are much appreciated.

A page from Miss Hull's photo album. The group is clearly marked as being in Quetta although sadly no individuals are named. Perhaps Frank is pictured here.

On the whole the health of the Territorials was better than might have been expected from a large body of unacclimatised and inexperienced men, many of them young. At one time nearly 100 of the 2/4th were suffering from defective heart action, caused by hard work in an atmosphere as rarified as that of Quetta, but these men soon became fit again. Despite the air, 1,680m above sea level, and weather, freezing with snow or over 40C, we know that the battalion was very successful at station sports, football included. There were pantomimes and concerts and the 2/4th published a journal under the title *The Tiger*. No doubt Frank would have loved the football and the entertainments too, looking back at earlier Twyford performances. But it was short-lived. Six months after his arrival and a couple of weeks before his 20th birthday, he died from diphtheria in the station hospital. No doubt today's antibiotics would have saved him.

He was awarded the British War medal and was buried in the Quetta government cemetery in the Baleli Road. His name is inscribed on the Lutyens-designed India Gate in Delhi, face 23. Friends visiting India recently, tracked it down and photographed his inscription for this project. His memorial service was held in

Twyford on 11 July 1915 attended by parents, relatives and many friends; Miss Hull and the members of St Mary's Bible Class were also present.

India Gate in Delhi, initially known as the All India War Memorial

Miss Leila Hull in the garden of her home, Monks Barn

The following week Col Yorke took the Church Lads' Brigade parade. He was much grieved to hear of Frank's death, who had been such a credit to the company since 1911 and from whom he had recently received a letter. Mr and Mrs Dumper moved to Hockley Cottages. Frank's sister Elsie lived there too with her husband Chris Pearce. She died in 1976 in her sleep, after a whist drive at the fire station.

The 2/4th Hants spent two years as a depot battalion stationed at Quetta, continually exchanging men with the 1/4th in Mesopotamia (now covering parts of Iraq and Syria) with many convalescent wounded returning to Quetta. In 1917 they were sent to Egypt for the final part of the Palestine expedition ending in the capture of Jerusalem. They subsequently served on the Western Front during the final advance resulting in the Armistice of 11 November 1918.

Jane Beljic

A poem by Lt G Elton (part) from "The Tiger" May 1915 seemed to say it all.

June in Hampshire

In Quetta lamps are lighted
And like a sound in dreams,
The bugle calls at evening
Across the seven streams,
How sweet and faint it seems.

O, here I am a soldier
And here my heart must stay
Till twilight's in the barracks
And with the end of day
My heart is far away.

For Hannah pass is rocky
And high is Murdar Hill
But O for June in Hampshire
And the fields my people till
My heart is crying still.

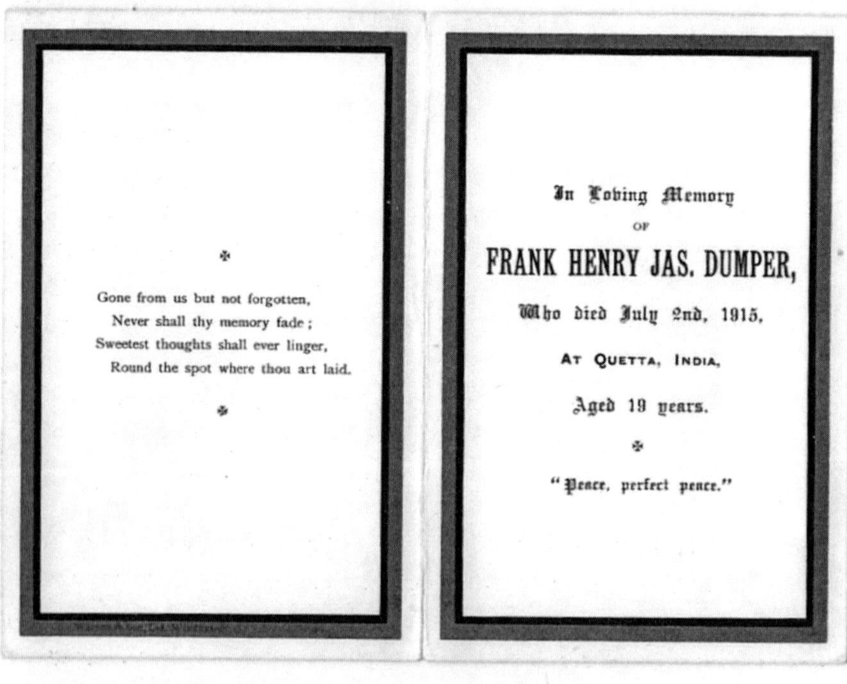

Alfred J Higgins

Private Alfred John Higgins Hampshire Regiment (January 1897 - 21 August 1915)

Alfred John Higgins was born in Kings Cross in London in January 1897, the son of Frederick Charles Higgins and Lillian May Higgins (nee Mills).

His parents had married in October 1892 at St James Parish Church Clerkenwell. Frederick was 25 and a glasscutter. Lillian May Mills was 19, her father George who came from Longparish and had been a publican in Bransbury had already died, her mother was Hannah (or Anna) Mills. At the time of the 1891 census Hannah Mills was the publican of the Bricklayer's Arms in Middle Brook Street in Winchester, and Lillian May, then 18 and described as a Mother's Help, was living with her and with her three younger siblings.

In the 1901 census Frederick Charles and Lillian May Higgins were living in St James parish Finsbury with Alfred and his elder sister, Jessie, born in 1894. Frederick Charles Higgins died the following year. It seems likely that Lillian moved back to Winchester after her husband's death, for in 1903 she married Thomas Taylor who came from Crewkerne. They married in St Thomas' Parish Church in Winchester on 2 August 1903. The 1911 census finds Thomas and Lillian May Taylor living at Kings Croft, Kings Road, Swanage. He was 31 and a Butcher's Assistant, she was 37. Alfred John, then 14 and a News Boy, was living with them, as was his younger full sister, Lillian Anne aged 9, and the three children of that marriage.

Alfred John Higgins was thus 17 and a half when the First World War broke out in August 1914. The 10th Battalion The Hampshire Regiment was raised in Winchester in the same month as part of Kitchener's First New Army and moved to Dublin to join 10th (Irish) Division. They returned to England in May 1915 and underwent final training in Basingstoke. The battalion was destined to join the Mediterranean Expeditionary Force for the Dardanelles Campaign, the venture seeking to bypass the stalemate on the Western Front by attacking Turkey at Gallipoli, aiming to knock them out of the war. While Alfred's regimental number, 14636, suggests that he joined up in November 1914, it would seem more likely that he joined in that short period when the battalion returned to England.

The battalion sailed for Gallipoli from Liverpool in the SS Transylvania on 6 July 1915. During the early part of the voyage vigilance had to be kept for submarines. On 26 July they landed at the port of Mudros on the Greek island of Lemnos. Cramped conditions during the voyage meant that their physical fitness had suffered, but they were to be fighting in the arduous terrain of the peninsular. The plan was that the battalion should land North of Cape Hellas at Suvla Bay. On 5 August they embarked on small boats to be landed under cover of darkness.

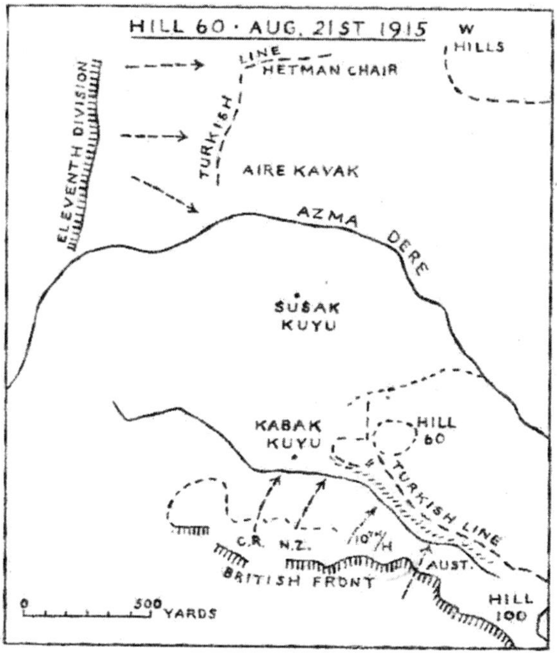

Map showing position of 10th Bn (10TH/H) and Hill 60[1]

During the fierce fighting over the coming days, between 5 and 21 August the 10th Hampshires suffered many casualties. Alfred John Higgins died on 21 August: whether from wounds earlier received or during a fierce engagement attacking a position called Hill 60 is unclear from the records.

On 29/30 September the battalion was evacuated to Mudros, due to heavy losses from combat, disease and severe weather conditions. He is commemorated on the Helles Memorial, *"Private Alfred Higgins 14636, 10th Bn. Hampshire Regiment who died on 21 August 1915 was aged 18, he was the son of Mrs Lillian May Taylor of Ashley, Twyford, Winchester"*.

Thomas Taylor and his wife bought Ashley in Finches Lane in November 1919, the conveyance records them as already of that address; the likelihood is that they were then tenants of the house. They were certainly in Twyford in 1918: Lillian's daughter Jessie Mabel Higgins, Alfred's elder sister, was married in Twyford Church on 4 May 1918 to Thomas Henry Anderson of Trowbridge.

The character of the front window of Ashley suggests that it was once a butchers' shop front. Trade Directories show butchers in Twyford from 1915: "W Taylor English and Colonial Meat Stores, High Street". One must assume W Taylor was some relation of Thomas's.

Whether Alfred John Higgins ever was in Twyford himself is unclear, though at the War's end his family would rightly have wished him to be remembered in what was then their village. Although not mentioned in the original paperwork or design for the memorial, his name was added at the bottom of the right-hand panel.

Alfred was awarded the 1915 Star, the British Medal and the Victory Medal.

Sue Kennedy.

Reference

1. Regimental History: The Royal Hampshire Regiment, Volume II 1914-1918, CT Atkinson, printed by Robert MacLehose & Company Limited, 1952, page 105.

Ashley, in Finches Lane, circa 1916

Geo Rainier Crawford

Colonel George Rainier Crawford CB Duke of Wellingtons Regiment (28 May 1862 – 22 August 1915)

Early Life and Family

George Rainier Crawford was born on 28 May 1862 in Murree, in the Punjab area of India.

Murree, located on the southern slopes of the Western Himalayan foothills, was the summer capital of the Punjab Province of British India until 1864. The town was originally established in 1850 as a sanatorium for British troops garrisoned on the Afghan frontier. The church there was consecrated in May 1857, where George's parents, Francis Haden Crawford and Eliza Priscilla Smith, were married on 12 November 1859. He was a Captain in the 98th Regiment of Foot and was, at the time, based in Peshawar. The regiment had been one of the first British units to serve on the North West Frontier and had, in 1858, been employed as part of the Sittana Field Force sent to deal with the so-called Hindustani Fanatics. Both Francis and Eliza came from military families: Francis' father, George Crawford (1776-1847), had been a major general in the Royal Artillery. Eliza's father, Matthew Smith (1797-1875), was a major general in 1862 and was promoted to lieutenant general and colonel of the 76th Regiment of Foot in 1871.

George had two siblings: Isabella, born in Murree in 1861 and a younger brother, Francis Haden. He was born in 1864, shortly after the death of their father in Ambala (Umballa), and named after him.

After the death of her young husband – he was only 44 years old – Eliza Crawford returned to England with her children to live, initially, with her father at 18 Scarsdale Villas in Kensington. They were living there for the 1871 census.

Life in the Army

George Crawford passed the qualifying examination for a cadetship at the Royal Military College, Sandhurst in August 1880. He was commissioned into the South Staffordshire Regiment (80th Foot) on 22 October 1881. In January 1882, George was sent to Malla in India with his regiment. However, in March 1882 he was transferred to the 2nd Battalion, 'King's Own' Royal Lancaster Regiment who were also serving in India. In 1885 he was seconded for service with the Indian Staff Corps. The term "Staff Corps" in an Indian context is not the same as that in other armies of the period (i.e. composed of Staff Officers). Following the take-over of the Honourable East India Company armies by the Crown, after the Mutiny, Staff Corps were just "pools" of officer manpower from which individuals could be drawn to fill vacancies in regiments or for detachment to assist the civil government or local police forces.

According to George Crawford's brief obituary, published in Twyford's Parish Magazine, George "took part in the Sushai Expedition of 1881 (n.b. this should read Lushai Expedition of 1889), and in the Hazara Expedition of 1891, when he received the medal with clasp. He was also engaged in the operations on the North West Frontier of India in 1897-8, again receiving a medal with clasp. Further action came on the North-Western Frontier in 1908, when he was mentioned in despatches and received the medal with clasp." Crawford's entry in *"Who's Who"* is clearer about the expeditions with which he was involved; a few notes on some of these follow below.

Lushai, 1889

In 1889 the British military organised a punitive expedition, named the Chin-Lushai Expeditionary Force, to supress rebellious tribes in the Chin Hills in central Burma, 150 miles to the east of Chittagong. It was divided into two columns: the Chittagong column occupied most of the southern region, including the Chin Hills, by the end of 1889 and the Cachar column camped at Aizawl on 30 January 1890. They defeated all the major chiefdoms, captured the chiefs and established permanent fortifications in Aizawl and Lunglei, as the administrative centres.

Hazara, 1891

The Hazara Expedition of 1891 was staged against the Hassanzais and Akazais in the Black Mountain area, in the Hindu Kush Mountains on the North-West Frontier, during the period 12 March to 16 May 1891. The objectives of the British operations were to assert their right to move along the crest of the Black Mountain; punishing the clans that had recently shown hostility to a force under Sir John McQueen; and to occupy the country until their complete submission had been achieved. It was decided that Oghi, Tilli and Pabal Gali would be occupied.

Little opposition was experienced until the 19 March when a British outpost was attacked violently by the tribesmen. Small engagements occurred near Palosi on the right bank and later at Kanhar, Diliarai (near Bakrai) and Darbanai on the left bank during a methodical advance up the Indus. In April the operations were extended eastwards from Bakrai into the heart of the Black Mountain. The brief campaign came to an end on the 17 April 1891 and within the next fortnight the tribesmen made their submission and accepted the terms imposed on them.

Tirah, 1897

The Tirah Expedition, was an Indian frontier war of 1897–1898. Tirah is a mountainous tract of country in what is now the tribal areas of Pakistan and includes the Khyber Pass. The Afridi tribe had for sixteen years received a subsidy from the government of British India for safeguarding the Khyber Pass, in addition to which the government had maintained for this purpose a local regiment entirely composed of Afridis, who were stationed in the pass. Suddenly, however, the tribesmen rose, captured all the posts in the Khyber held by their own countrymen, and attacked the forts on the Samana Range near the city of Peshawar.

The frontier post of Kohat was selected as the base of the campaign and, on 18 October, the operations commenced, fighting ensuing immediately. The Dargai heights, which commanded the line of advance, were captured without difficulty, but abandoned owing to the want of water. On 20 October the same positions were stormed, with a loss of 199 of the British force killed and wounded.

The force, in detached brigades, now proceeded to traverse the Tirah district in all directions, and to destroy the walled and fortified hamlets of the Afridis. Almost daily the Afridis, too wise to risk general engagements, waged guerrilla warfare, and the various bodies of troops engaged in foraging or survey duties were constantly attacked. On 21 November, a brigade was detached to visit the Rajgul valley. The road was exceedingly difficult and steady opposition was encountered. However, the objectives were accomplished.

The army then prepared to evacuate Tirah, with the two divisions leaving by separate routes. The base was to be transferred from Kohat to Peshawar. The return march began on 9 December. The cold was intense, temperatures of -21^{0}C being registered before leaving Tirah. The movement of the first division though demanding was practically unopposed, but the 40 miles to be covered by the second division were contested almost throughout. The march down the Bara valley commenced on 10 December, and involved four days of the hardest fighting and marching of the campaign; not only were soldiers killed in attacks, but many died of exposure, and quantities of stores were lost. On the 14th a link with the Peshawar column was achieved. The first division, aided by the Peshawar column, now took possession of the Khyber forts without opposition.

Negotiations for peace were then begun with the Afridis who, under the threat of another expedition into Tirah in the spring, at length agreed to pay the fines and to surrender the rifles demanded. The expeditionary force was broken up on 4 April 1898.

By 1907, George Crawford had been promoted to lieutenant colonel and made Commandant of the 40th Pathans, the only all-Pathan regiment in the Indian Army, with the nickname of the "Forty Thieves".

Meanwhile...

At some point before 1881, Eliza Crawford, George's mother, moved with her daughter, Isabella, and younger son, Francis, to live in Cheltenham. She lived here until her death in 1908 at the age of 75.

Francis Crawford later returned to London to run a small School in Uxbridge – Scarsdale School – probably named after the road in Kensington the family had lived in following their return to the United Kingdom.

Isabella Crawford trained and found employment as a nurse in Cheltenham. By 1901 she was Assistant Superintendent and Secretary to the District Nursing Association, and was working at the Victoria Home in St. James' Square, Cheltenham. Her superior at the Victoria Home and Superintendent of the District Nursing Association was Katherine Maude Bladen. Katherine was born in Hanley, Staffordshire in 1862.

Marriage

In 1907 George travelled from India to Britain to see his family and on 17 September he married Katherine Bladen at All Saints Church in Cheltenham. According to the *"Cheltenham Looker-On"*, which carried news of the wedding, Lt Col and Mrs Crawford then proceeded directly to India to take up residence in Jelum.

In the following year, George was then involved in more fighting on the North West Frontier for which he was Mentioned in Despatches.

In June 1909 he was promoted to brevet colonel and, on 1 January 1911, full colonel.

One year later, George was still in India and is mentioned in the Indian Army Quarterly List. However, in 1913 he retired from the Indian Army and was appointed Companion of The Most Honourable Order of the Bath (CB).

Twyford and the Later Years

George and Katherine returned to Cheltenham. Later they moved to Twyford purchasing 'The Mount', a house in Roman Road. How long they were actually there is unclear, but George became involved in the local community and was elected a sidesman at St Mary's Church.

Great Britain declared war on Germany on 4 August 1914. Soon afterwards George applied for reinstatement to the Army, only to be deemed unfit for active service.

The Mount in Roman Road, Twyford, 2018

However, a month later he was appointed Honorary Colonel of the newly-formed 10th Battalion Duke of Wellington's (West Riding) Regiment. The battalion was in training at Frensham, near Aldershot. One report from a member of the battalion said that Crawford, *"inspires confidence, and takes a deep interest in the men individually."* The battalion continued their training in Aldershot (December 1914), Folkestone (February 1915) and Bramshott (May 1915).

Sadly at this stage George's health deteriorated and he was replaced by Lieutenant Colonel Hugh Bartholomew as Commanding Officer of the 10th Battalion on 4 May 1915. He returned to The Mount in Twyford and, in the words of the Parish Magazine, *"after some months of failing strength, born with a quiet and patient courage, he fell asleep on Sunday August 22"*. The cause of death, as stated on his death certificate, was arteriosclerosis (the thickening, hardening and loss of elasticity of the walls of arteries), cardiac hypertrophy (a thickening of the heart muscle which results in a decrease in size of the chamber of the heart) and cardiac failure. He was buried in the churchyard of St. Peter's Church, Leckhampton just outside Cheltenham on 26 August 1915. He was 53.

George's widow, Katherine, returned to Cheltenham, living at 2 Beechworth Villas, Hale's Road. She continued to live in Cheltenham until her death in 1937.

Andrew Keeling.

George Crawford's medals - comprising The Most Honourable Order of the Bath, Companion's breast badge, India General Service Medal, two clasps, Lushai 1889-92 and Hazara 1891, India Medal, two clasps Punjab Frontier 1897-98 and Tirah 1897-98, India General Service Medal, one clasp North West Frontier 1908 and Delhi Durbar Medal 1903, 40th Pathans helmet plate and cap badge and silver chains, boss and whistle.

The Webb Brothers, Mark and Walter George

Sergeant Walter George Webb Wiltshire Regiment (14 April 1879 - 1 September 1915) and Stoker First Class Mark Webb RN HMTB 96 (23 February 1883 - 1 November 1915)

Walter and Mark came from a large family. Their father Batholomew was a farmworker from central Hampshire who had married Sarah Hack. They came from Mottisfont and moved around following work as opportunity arose.

They had ten children in all, Thomas, Mary, James, Frank, Harry, Walter, George, Mark, William and Kate. Their birthplaces catalogue local villages that we recognise Broughton, Kimpton, Romsey, Ovington, Headbourne Worthy, Putley and Alresford among others. Walter was born on 14 April 1879 in Headbourne Worthy. Sarah is recorded as working in 'Domestic Service' at the time. Mark was born on 23 February 1883 in Ovington. The expectation for the boys was doubtless that they would follow their father into working on the land.

When Walter and Mark were just nine and five their father died, aged 44, so times must have been very tough for Sarah, and indeed the family, with no main breadwinner. Three years later Sarah was living in Kimpton, just the other side of Andover, with the seven younger children. The two boys were at school there.

The census of 1881 shows eldest brother Thomas, aged 13, working as a 'Ploughboy'; this brings to mind the picture by George Clausen, Ploughing (1889), of the boy leading the horse as his father manages the plough. It's a dour, grey day, the nearer horse is distinctly bony and the boy appears to be clad in a hessian sack as his main protection against the weather, a tough life. Was this Thomas' lot? Were Walter and Mark destined to follow in these footsteps?

By 1901 the family had moved to Twyford, where Sarah was living with her younger children in Park Lane. The puzzle for me about Sarah is that she appears to have changed her name to Spicer although I have been unable to find any record of a marriage to Mr Spicer. Sarah died in 1911 and was buried in St Mary's churchyard on 19 October aged 65. The small mercy is that she was never to know of the loss of two of her boys, just two months apart, in the war that was to come.

Mark however had left home, he was living in Tandridge in Surrey, just outside East Grinstead. He was working as a cattle stockman on a local farm and lodging with Lydia Friend, a widow, at Wenders Hill Castle Cottage. [At this point a discrepancy about his age creeps in, which is perpetuated in later documents. The 1901 census reports him as being 16, although having been born in February 1883 he would have been 18.]

Walter George Webb

Walter also went on to work on the land. Furthermore, in 1910 he got married, to Alice Louisa Withers. The service was in our St Mary's Church, on 9 November. Alice's family came from Berkshire with connections in Newbury (perhaps this is why Walter headed for the Wiltshire Regiment when the time came). Both bride and groom gave their residence as Twyford and both were aged 31. At this time Walter was working as a Dairyman.

The following year they were living at Bryn Bank in the village. He was a 'Labourer in Mill', I wonder what might have happened to his previous job as a Dairyman, in those days job security was not to be taken for granted. Also with him and Alice on Census night was Harriet Bridges, recorded as a Visitor. Perhaps a friend or lodger helping to contribute to a stretched budget. None of them is mentioned on the Electoral Roll of that year.

Their first daughter, Amy Louisa, was born on 17 August 1913. Walter was now working as a Labourer. Second daughter Kathleen Mary arrived almost two years later, on 13 June 1915, by which time Walter had enlisted and already a sergeant in the Wiltshire Regiment.

When war came ... Walter enlisted at Salisbury. We don't know exactly when this was, a large proportion of the War Department's service records were destroyed in the blitz, known as the 'burnt records', it very much looks as though Walter's were among these. My feeling is that Walter didn't enlist immediately, he doesn't appear in the initial Parish Magazines of August and September 1914 recording those who volunteered straightaway and as a family man in his mid-thirties he may have felt under less pressure.

However it cannot have been long before he enrolled and was assigned to the 1st Battalion, it was a regular battalion, part of 7th Brigade within the 3rd Division.

> *"Based in Southern Command when the war broke out in August 1914, the units making up 3rd Division were dispatched to France to join the British Expeditionary Force. As part of II Corps, they were all ashore by 16th August 1914 and went straight up to the front at Mons. Taking up positions along the Mons-Conde canal, the division gave a good account of itself (the first three VCs of the war were won by men from the division on this day), but at high costs - more than 3,000 casualties. The retreat followed, along with service on the Aisne before moving up to French Flanders in early October 1914 to take part in the fighting south of Armentières. It was here, on October 14th at Vielle Chapelle, that the division's first commander, Major General H.I.W.Hamilton was killed. By the end of November 1914 the division as a whole had suffered 8,355 casualties since mid-October: from this it is possible to gauge the ferocity of the fighting.*
>
> *In early 1915 the division moved up to the Ypres Salient, and took over the trenches opposite the Messines Ridge, and at St Eloi and The Bluff. 3rd Division then moved up to the Menin Road sector at Hooge and Bellewaarde and fought actions there on 16th June and 25th September 1915 - losing 5,600 men."*[1]

By this time Walter had been made up to sergeant, from comments in the War Diary, it looks as though he was in B Company. We don't know whether he was at home for the birth of Kathleen Mary, perhaps he had managed to get leave and avoided the heavy actions in the battalion's sector in mid-June, in any event he survived them and was with the battalion through August. We do know that Walter was killed on the first of September 1915 when the battalion was at Hooge in Belgium. This small village lies on the Ypres to Menin road; Dickebusche (or Dikkebus) is just over six miles southwest from Hooge and Poperinghe is a few miles northwest, the area is noted for hop growing and lace production. The following extracts from the battalion war diary give a record of what were to be Walter's last days.

> *27th August HOOGE The battalion was relieved by RIR (Royal Irish Rifles) and returned to bivouacs NW of Dickebusche. Casualties 1 Killed 7 Wounded.*
>
> *28th August NW DICKEBUSCHE Resting. Fine.*

29th August NW DICKEBUSCHE Resting. Voluntary church parade with band. Wet afternoon. Coys (Companies) marched to POPERINGHE to bathe.

30th August NW DICKEBUSCHE Rain most of the day. Battalion marched to HOOGE in the evening and relieved RIR. B Coy garrisoned Crater trenches. Relief completed 1 am. Casualties 1 Killed 1 Wounded.

31st August HOOGE Quiet day. Work was done in the advanced trench around the stables & in 1st retrenchment. At one point the German trenches run very close to ours; parties of the enemy were observed putting out barbed wire. Some was laid on our own parapet by the Germans who approached within 2 yards of our advanced posts. They were apparently not aware that we held it. Orders had been given not to fire and attract attention, as our working parties were digging in very exposed places. Casualties 1 Wounded.

September 1st HOOGE Our heavy artillery bombarded German lines from daylight to 4.30 am. Enemy retaliated by shelling heavily Crater and surrounding trenches. Trenches were very much damaged. All telephone lines to the front trenches were cut. Communications trenches were blown in places, and supports shelled. Casualties 4 Killed 26 Wounded. [2]

On the following day a more intense artillery duel occurred. The battalion called up Corps level batteries. The butchers roll for the day amounted to 14 Killed, 38 Wounded, two Missing believed killed. The following day was quiet, three wounded only, and the battalion received from General Haldane the following message "Convey to Wiltshire regiment my appreciation of stout-hearted manner they stood bombardment yesterday. Regret heavy casualties."[3]

So died Walter, a casualty not of a great set-piece battle, but of the continuous daily grind of artillery duels and trench warfare along the Western Front, low-level activity punctuated by occasional flare-ups, but all none the less deadly. Bad news travels fast, his death was announced in the October edition of the Parish Magazine.

Walter is buried in Belgium with 453 others in the 'La Brique Military Cemetery No.2' in West-Vlaanderen now just north of Ypres, now between the golf course and a hospital. The Medal Roll records his receipt of the 1914-15 Star, the War Medal and the Victory Medal.

Mark Webb

On the 8 June in 1903, when he was 20, Mark left his job on the land and travelled to Portsmouth to enlist in the Navy. He signed on for twelve years. At the time he had been working as a cowman and his papers show that he had brown hair, grey eyes and a fresh complexion, he was 5 feet 2¼ inches tall with a couple of scars on his left forearm.

His first posting was to HMS Nelson, an old armoured cruiser from the era of sail and steam, three-masted but with two steam engines. In 1902 she had been converted to a training ship for stokers and Mark learned his trade on her. The role of the stoker was to shovel the coal used to fire the ship's boilers. Later, and as oil replaced coal as the power source, and in more senior roles, stokers carried out the multiplicity of maintenance tasks required in the ship's engine room.

After training Mark was posted to HMS Firequeen, formerly a steam yacht but now being used for general purposes around Portsmouth and the Isle of Wight. She was a general depot ship and used occasionally for ceremonial duties, such as meeting foreign royalty arriving in their own yachts and providing a luxury taxi service for Royals and VIPs to and from the Isle of Wight.

Mark's service record shows a total of 16 postings over his twelve-year service. Some are quite short, that to HMS Hermione in July 1905 was for 11 days. She was an Astraea-class, 10-gun twin-screw cruiser of 4,360 tons.

Then for six months in 1905 to HMS Vulcan. She was a torpedo boat depot ship of 6,820 tons. The increasing numbers of torpedo boats which had entered service had generated the need for specialist support ships. Vulcan could carry six torpedo boats on her deck and had repair workshops and equipment stores. A posting to the depot ship could equally mean assignment to one of the smaller vessels that were the responsibility of the mother ship. This looks like Mark's first assignment to this type of small craft.

Late in 1906 he was made up to a Stoker First Class. Throughout his naval service, annually, he received a VG (Very Good) assessment of 'Character'.

His next posting was similar, to HMS Leander, another depot ship, for torpedo boat destroyers. She served with the Mediterranean Fleet providing a base for up to 21 TBDs.

Come 1910 a change, Mark was posted for 14 months to HMS Venerable (1899), a London-class pre-dreadnought battleship. She had just had a major refit. He was on her on Census night in 1911 when she was at Gibraltar, assigned to the Atlantic Fleet. The census return reports her total crew strength as 694. Mark's status at the time was shown as 'Single' and religion 'Ch. of England'.

Further postings came thick and fast, four months in 1912 to HMS Arrogant, a second class cruiser launched in 1896. She was used as a depot ship from 1911 and was sold in 1923.

In 1912-13 his posting was to HMS Dolphin, another depot ship. In the War she was to be used as a submarine tender. Later in 1913 to HMS Cormorant, she was an old sloop, 1877, and used as the receiving ship at Gibraltar. He was posted on 8 October 1913 and so would have been in Gibraltar when war broke out. He was assigned to the Local Defence Flotilla, comprising a group of torpedo boats, numbers 83 and 88-97. The flotilla was responsible for escort and protection duties for larger units of the fleet. Mark's boat was TB96, she was 140 feet long and displaced 130 tons. She was built at Whites Shipyard at Cowes on the Isle of Wight and launched in 1894. She was armed with three three-pounder guns and mounted three 14-inch torpedo tubes. Chief Gunner John Sumner was in command.

HM Torpedo Boat 96

When war came, one of the principal duties of the TBs was patrolling the Straits of Gibraltar to counter the German submarine threat. The patrols would have been particularly required at night, and it was early in the morning of Monday 1 November that no. 96 was out on patrol five miles east of Gibraltar. The record does not describe the weather conditions, but it would have been dark when a deadly collision occurred. TB 96 ahd been run down by a much larger vessel. The SS Tringa was a Fleet Auxiliary, one of many merchant ships drafted to meet the logistical needs of the fleet. She displaced 2,154 tons, ie almost twenty times as big as the little TB 96. The torpedo boat couldn't have lasted long. Of her 18 man crew 11, including the captain, were lost. Perhaps the seven survivors were picked up by the Tringa, once she had realised what she had done.

SS Tringa, shortly before her launching on the Tyne in 1913

Although the SS Tringa survived the collision, she herself was lost at the hand of a U-boat shortly after. On 26 November she was captured by U-33 thirty miles from Galata Island (the Galite islands, 24 miles off the coast of Tunisia, towards Sardinia) and sunk by gunfire, with the loss of three lives[4].

Despite the fact that this was war, the loss of TB 96 did not go unrecorded locally. There is a memorial in Gibraltar's North Front Cemetery to "the eleven very gallant sailors of H.M.'s Torpedo Boat 96" and Mark's name is there. His name also appears on the Royal Navy's Memorial at Southsea overlooking the Solent.

Memorial in Gibraltar to crew of TB 96

The naval medal record shows that Mark received the 1914 Star, the Victory Medal and the War Medal, they were sent to his brother. A final and local detail is revealed in the administration of Mark's will, granted probate on 24 June 1916. Giving his own address as School Road, Twyford, he left his effects and estate, valued at £95 0s. 6d. to his brothers Thomas Bartholomew, carter, and Frank, gardener, who were both living in School Road at the time.

When they died, Walter was 36 and Mark 32.

Christopher Pope

References:

1. British Infantry Divisions of The Great War 1914-1918, Short Histories by Paul Reed (http://battlefields1418.50megs.com/divisions1.htm).
2. War Diary, 1st Bn Wiltshire Regiment, National Archives, Ref WO/95/1415/0/302.
3. Sir James Aylmer Lowthorpe Haldane GCMG, KCB, DSO (1862-1950), GOC 3rd Division (Wikipedia).
4. Extracted from: "World War 1 at Sea - Royal Navy Vessels Lost and Damaged", enlarged and corrected version of the original HMSO, "British Vessels Lost at Sea 1914-1918" - October - December 1915 by Gordon Smith, Naval-History.Net

School Road, with pupils outside the school

Jack Stanley Powell

Private Jack Stanley Powell Hampshire Regiment (19 October 1896 - 8 October 1915)

It is 22 July 1894 and in St Michael's Church, in the gloriously named Cotswold village of Duntisbourne Rouse in Gloucestershire (population then 120), a mile or so north-west of Cirencester, a young woman is sitting in Church waiting for the service to start. She is admiring the herringbone masonry on the north side of the nave, the blocked rectangular door and the Norman Chancel arch, for this is an old building, the oldest parts are Anglo-Saxon, the chancel was added by the Normans in the 12th century, and so was a tiny crypt below it. In the 15th century they put up a little tower but not much has changed since then. Simon Jenkins[1] was to write *"Every now and again I come across a church where I think 'this is a place I could imagine being buried when I die'. For me Duntisbourne Rouse is such a church ... the sort of places which, when we see them on a lovely sunny day, make us feel that there is really nowhere in the world to match Britain at its best."*

Kate Ada Boulton has come to Church for the first reading of her banns. She is to marry Thomas Powell from Hampshire and to embark on a marriage that would lead to her outliving both her husband and their son Jack. The marriage took place later that summer.

They returned to live in Hampshire, to the family home in Alresford, somewhat later recorded as Langtons Cottages[2], although Thomas was the butler at Twyford Lodge some ten miles away. Jack was born there two years later, on the 19 October 1896. The christening was held in the town at St John the Baptist Church on 7 January 1897.

Thomas' job had moved on by 1901. The Lodge had changed hands and there is no record of him there.

Sadly tragedy was to strike the family in 1909 when Thomas died. He was 47, Jack was just 12. Thomas was buried in the Churchyard at St John's on 27 January. This was clearly a blow that seems to have broken up the family, because two years later Jack was living in Shawford with his uncle and aunt's family, the Hawkins. Perhaps this connection was on his mother's side as John Thomas' wife Annie Elizabeth and their eldest daughter Florence Annie were both recorded on the Census form then as being born in Cirencester. Anyway at this time Jack was 14 and still at school. They lived just inside the parish boundary in the Mill House, by the bridge. John

Thomas was the miller and ran a small dairy farm and although his son Wilfred was recorded as the 'Dairy Farm Helper', the whole family, Jack included, would have been involved in working with the cattle and the business.

The Mill at Shawford

This looks a happy period in Jack's life; over the next few years he is mentioned five times in the parish magazine, clearly well established in the community. On 17 April 1914 he took part in a Young Helpers League[3] concert at the Parish Hall. He was one of a cast of 21, their piece being "A Dissatisfied Fairy". The event raised £3/0/0. He was also a member of Miss Hull's Bible Class, formed in 1913 – 36 members of the class signed up in the course of the war, nine were not to return.

On leaving school Jack went to work for Messrs James Harris and Son; they were auctioneers in Jewry Chambers in Winchester and he started out as a clerk.

When war broke out Jack was still only 17. It looks as though he signed up as soon as he was 18. Readers will recollect that the greater proportion of the Army's enlistment and personnel records were destroyed in the blitz so we have no military record of Jack signing up. In November 1914 however the parish magazine records that Jack is 'Serving King and Country' in the Hampshire Regiment (T.F.) [Territorial Force]. Six months later the magazine again mentions Jack being in the military, having responded to the "call to serve" and in August 1915 the magazine publishes a long list of those serving, and Jack is confirmed as being in the Hampshire Regiment.

We have a couple of sources for Jack's battalion, one recording it as the 4th, or 1/4th, and another the 2/4th. We know that both the 4th battalions were sent to India, the 1/4th Battalion landed at Karachi in November 1914 and the 2/4th Battalion sailed for India in December 1914. The Bible Class roll records Jack being in the 2/4th and photos in Miss Hull's album show Jack in tropical kit, with pith helmet; it does look as though Jack did get to India, leaving a matter of weeks after his 18th birthday.

Jack Stanley Powell – from Miss Hull's Photo Album

However only ten months later Jack was back in England where sadly he died on 8 October 1915. At this time his battalion is recorded as being the 84th Provisional Battalion. The Provisional Battalions were formed of men from the 2nd and 3rd line battalions who were not available for overseas service due to age or health conditions and the 84th had been formed in June 1915 from "Home Service only" personnel. They were grouped into Provisional Brigades along with newly formed companies of Royal Engineers, ASC, Artillery with Ammunition Column, a Yeomanry Squadron and a Field Ambulance unit. In the strategic scheme of things these battalions were designated to Home Defence and Jack would have been involved in protecting key installations and the coastline.

So in the course of a very few months it seems that Jack travelled to India, perhaps caught a tropical disease and was returned to the UK, recovering a measure of health to enable him to be posted to the 84th Provisional, but subsequently to die eleven days before his nineteenth birthday. This is one scenario supported by the two photos of him with a pith helmet, alternatively he never left the UK and the photos were taken in a studio with some handy props and perhaps for health reasons he was diverted to the Provisional battalion. In either event this battalion was initially posted to Edinburgh and then to Newcastle. It was here that Jack became seriously ill and died, in the 1st Northern General Hospital[4]. His death certificate gives cause of death as "(1) Bronchiectasis (2) Empyema Pulmonary Endocarditis and Pericarditis P.M.". Jack's condition generally amounted to inflammation and infection of the lungs, bronchial tubes and linings of the heart and their combination presented a difficult challenge for treatment particularly in the pre antibiotic era. The condition was not inconsistent with contraction by natural causes, particularly if exposed to unhealthy living conditions, although the Hampshire Chronicle were later to report that Jack was "never of a very robust constitution".

The certificate gives "K. Powell, Mother" as informant, so clearly Kate had travelled to Newcastle to be with her son, hopefully she made it before he died. His civil address is given as The Mill, Shawford[5], so our local link continued to be important to Jack and the family.

Jack is recorded as a private. His name does not appear on the Medal Roll, confirming that he did not serve in a theatre of war. The 'Register of Soldiers' Effects' shows that seven shillings was paid to Kate on 5 May in 1916.

Jack's body was brought back to Alresford for burial in the Churchyard at St John's Church, on 13 October 1915. The Hampshire Chronicle of 16 October includes a formal notice of his death on page 5 and on page 6 no less than nine column inches describing the funeral. "*Impressive scenes were witnessed in the town on Wednesday when full military honours were accorded the mortal remains of the late Private Jack Stanley Powell.*" The body was met by a large unit of the Durham Light Infantry stationed in the town, the band of the 4th Hampshires had come up from Lyndhurst and another of the camps in the area had provided a carriage and gun drawn by seven horses to bear the coffin, draped with a Union Flag, with Jack's head-dress and side arms placed on top. Once the coffin had been lowered, the firing party fired three volleys over the grave and the 'Last Post' was sounded. There was a large number of mourners at the grave, including his mother, Kate Ada, younger brother James, uncle, aunt and cousins from Shawford, colleagues from James Harris and "a large number of local residents". There was a long list of those sending floral tributes, including Miss Hull, from Twyford, Lt Col Peters and all the men of the 84th Provisional Battalion, and others.

An impressive scene indeed - might this full scale funeral for a solitary boy in a quiet country churchyard have been an attempt to compensate for the hundreds of thousands of others who had died with no such recognition. Perhaps in death Jack had become a proxy for so many of those for whom family, friends and colleagues would never be able to pay their last respects.

Jack was buried in the same plot as his father, Thomas. His War Graves Commission headstone now stands within the surround which records, on opposite sides, both father and son.

Michael Andrews
Christopher Pope

References and Notes:

1. Simon Jenkins: Journalist, broadcaster and author. Edited the Times and the London Evening Standard and chaired the National Trust.
2. There is a Langtons Court in the town now, over the railway line off Sun Lane. Perhaps the cottages were a precursor to this.
3. Young Helpers League. The Young Helpers' League was founded by Dr Thomas Barnardo in 1891. It was one of the first schemes for mass charity giving - with much of the money for his children's homes and other projects coming in small amounts from a large number of donors. The subscription (in 1892) was sixpence - paid in stamps. The League encouraged more fortunate children to donate money and time to those less privileged. Its membership had grown to over 34,000 when Barnardo died in 1905.
4. 1st Northern General Hospital was one of the Territorial Army General Hospitals mobilised in August 1914. The buildings of Armstrong College, Durham University, now Newcastle University, and several others in the proximity, were requisitioned for the purpose. Initially established with 520 beds, this rose to 1,286 by August 1917. The hospital admitted 5,271 patients in 1914, 13,909 in 1915 and 11,804 in 1916.
5. Then, as today, The Mill at Shawford was often locally referred to as being in Shawford, although the parish boundary is down the centre of the main flow of the Itchen to the west of the mill, so that officially it is within the Parish of Twyford.

Thomas Mostyn Field

Midshipman Thomas Mostyn Field HMS Queen Mary (18 February 1900 - 31 May 1916)

Family and Early Life

Thomas Mostyn Field was born on 18 February 1900 in Brontëville, his parents' home in Merton Road, Southsea. The family were still there for the census in April 1901, when they are recorded as having three servants: a cook, a nurse and a housemaid.

Thomas' father, Admiral Sir Arthur Mostyn Field, KCB, FRS had a distinguished naval career. He had been Hydrographer of the Navy and had been elected a Fellow of the Royal Society in 1905. He also served as a churchwarden at Twyford Parish Church. He died on 3 July 1950 at his home, Rest Harrow in Woodgreen, Hants, shortly after his ninety-fifth birthday. Thomas' mother, Laura Mary Hale, was the daughter of Captain George Herbert Hale of the 57th Bengal Light Infantry. She was born in Brighton in 1865 and married Arthur Mostyn Field in March 1894. They had three children: Cecilia (1897-1992), Thomas and one other. Initially, the family home in Twyford was in "Searle's Hill", the building now used by Twyford School's Pre-Prep. They later moved to a house in Queen Street, referred to frequently in the parish magazines as being on the "left from High Street".

Thomas was educated at Twyford Preparatory School from 1909 until Christmas 1912. In January 1913 he entered the Royal Naval College, Osborne (in Osborne House on the Isle of Wight) and, after three years training, was appointed midshipman on HMS Queen Mary in January 1916, when he was still only 15. The Admiralty's view on boys serving in the war differed from the army where sixteen and seventeen-year-olds had to lie to join up and serve at the front. Boys had traditionally served on warships from the 17th century and as the fleet expanded in Victorian times the need for manpower meant that the navy couldn't be too scrupulous about age. Conditions had moved on from the 'powder monkeys' of Nelson's era and boy seamen, aged 15 - 17, were regarded as under training and expected to qualify in their chosen specialisation before being rated as an adult sailor. For the Midshipmen, expecting to qualify as officers, their seagoing time was also regarded as part of their training and they were required to study navigation, seamanship and other specialisations while undertaking regular duties, e.g. keeping watch and running the ship's boats. On HMS Queen Mary, for instance, the Chaplain's role included instruction of the junior officers.

On the declaration of war in 1914 any qualms about youthfulness were quashed, all the Dartmouth cadets were immediately mobilised, Churchill commenting:

> *"The decision to send the naval cadets ... to sea in time of war was arrived at a considerable time ago. It was felt that young officers of their age would be of great use on board His Majesty's ships, and that they would learn incomparably more of their profession in war than any educational establishment on shore could teach them."* [1]

Thomas Mostyn Field

So Thomas' posting to HMS Queen Mary at 15 years of age was very much part of the naval tradition. As a Midshipman Thomas lived in the Gun Room, the mess for cadets and other 'juniors'. In May he was joined there by Philip Malet de Carteret, two years older. Philip's letters to his father have recently been published, and in his last he describes the setting for this group of which Thomas was part:

"The Queen Mary is the most up to date ship. Among the many luxuries are a bath-room with hot water constantly laid on and two long baths. Also a cinema show to which I went last Thursday and it was quite decent. The Gunroom is well above the waterline (in the Canopus you could scarcely have the scuttles open at sea for fear of the water coming in) and contains a gramophone and a pianola. There are 25 of us in the Gunroom including 2 subs, an engineering sub and 2 clerks. All the rest of us are snotties[2], some junior and some senior to us."[3]

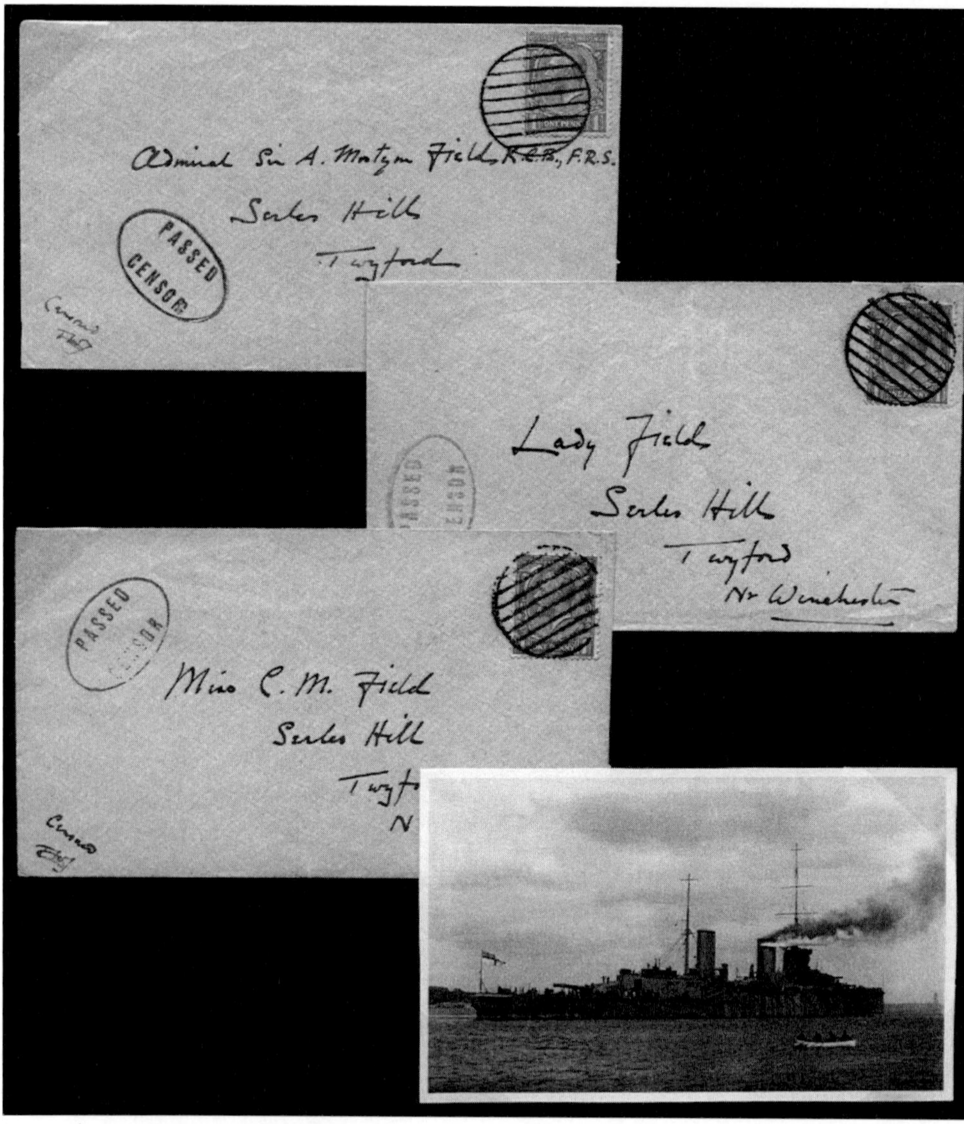

Letters Home from Thomas with picture of HMS Queen Mary

The Battle of Jutland

The Battle of Jutland is considered to be the only major naval battle of the First World War. It was generally believed that Britain had naval supremacy not only in Europe but also throughout the world. The British public had grown to believe that Britain could not be challenged when its navy was concerned. The song "Rule Britannia" was very much in this mould as the song starts "Rule Britannia, Britannia rules the waves, Britain never, never, never shall be slaves." A strong British navy was expected by the public, as was the inevitable naval victory.

At the start of the war, Britain was involved in two minor naval clashes – Heligoland and Dogger Bank. A full-scale naval clash between Germany and Britain had not occurred. Germany's fleet was smaller than Britain's but both fleets benefited from the development in 1906 of the Dreadnought. Overnight, all warships were redundant in terms of what they could do relative to the Dreadnought. The new design was quickly latched onto by the Germans and a naval race began.

Two fleets with such power could inflict great damage on the other. One argument that has been put forward for the lack of naval activity at the start of the war is that both fleets basically avoided a major clash for fear that it would be decisive and leave their respective nations vulnerable to attack.

The Royal Navy in the North Sea was based at Rosyth, Cromarty and Scapa Flow. Here it could protect the central and northern areas of the North Sea and stop the German High Seas Fleet from getting into the Atlantic where it could cause huge problems for Britain's merchant fleet. The British believed that the Germans would not try to rush the English Channel and face the might of the Navy based in Portsmouth and Plymouth. Therefore, it was reckoned that the German Navy could only operate in the North Sea.

The British had by 1916 put up an effective blockade of Germany. Germany's northern coastline was very small and any blockade was easy to enforce. Up to 1916, the German High Seas Fleet had been commanded by Admiral von Poul. He was considered to be too passive in his approach to what the German Navy could do. In 1916, von Poul was replaced by the far more aggressive Admiral Reinhardt von Scheer. He decided that the blockade had gone too far and was causing too much damage to Germany.

Scheer wanted to lure parts of the British fleet out of their respective naval bases and using a combination of submarines and surface boats attack and destroy them. On the night of the 24 and 25 April 1916, the German Navy attacked the coastal towns of Lowestoft and Yarmouth. The idea was that the British fleet would respond to this.

In May, Scheer ordered Admiral von Hipper to sea with 40 ships to move along the Danish coast. The news of this movement reached Admiral Jellicoe in Rosyth. He saw this movement of such a large force as provocative and ordered the Grand Fleet to put to sea. The Battle of Jutland started on 31 May 1916.

Locating the enemy's fleet proved a difficult task. Spotter reconnaissance planes were far too unreliable to cover the distance required over the North Sea. Therefore, fast cruisers (commanded by Captain - later Admiral - Edwyn Alexander-Sinclair, another former pupil of Twyford School) were sent out by both fleets to discover where the other was. When each did find the other there was a brief exchange of fire but both had done their task - hunting down the enemy.

Now that the British had found the Germans, Jellicoe was joined by the fleet based at Scapa Flow led by Sir David Beatty. Fifty-two ships joined the Grand Fleet. Jellicoe and Beatty faced a fleet of forty German ships led by Admiral Hipper. They opened fire at one another at a distance of about ten miles. Though they were a smaller force, the initial advantage lay with the Germans who were helped with their visibility by the lay of the sun.

Just after 16.00, the British battle cruiser "Indefatigable" was destroyed by the Germans. One thousand men lost their lives when a magazine exploded. Nearly thirty minutes later, "Queen Mary" was sunk in just ninety seconds.

Thomas Mostyn Field - Circumstances of Death

Extract from the Official History;

> *"... for Admiral Hipper was in action again. At 4.10, being then eleven miles away abaft the beam of the Lion, he inclined inwards a couple of points, and as Admiral Beatty simultaneously altered still more to port to press his van, he was able at 4.17 to re-open fire at extreme range. The Lion had not yet been able entirely to master the fire that was smothering her. To the Germans she must have been invisible, for the Derfflinger, mistaking the Princess Royal for the flagship, began firing on the next astern, which the Seydlitz was also engaging. Thus the Queen Mary, at from 15,800 to 14,500 yards, became the target of both these ships. For about five minutes she stood it gallantly. She was fighting splendidly. The Germans say full salvoes were coming from her with fabulous rapidity. Twice already she had been straddled by the Derfflinger, when at 4.26 a plunging salvo crashed upon her deck forward. In a moment there was a*

dazzling flash of red flame where the salvo fell, and then a much heavier explosion rent her amidships. Her bows plunged down, and as the Tiger and New Zealand raced by her to port and starboard, her propellers were still slowly revolving high in the air. In another moment, as her two consorts were smothered in a shower of black debris, there was nothing of her left but a dark pillar of smoke rising stem-like till it spread hundreds of feet high in the likeness of a vast palm tree. Two such successes were beyond anything the Germans had reason to expect. Admiral Scheer's plan had broken down, and yet they were gaining even more than he could have hoped for ..."[4]

An account of the loss of HMS Queen Mary, by the Navigating Officer of HMS New Zealand (4.26 pm, 31 May, 1916)

"All seemed to be going well with us on New Zealand when suddenly I saw a salvo hit Queen Mary on her port side. A small cloud of what looked like coal-dust came out from where she was hit, but nothing more until several moments later, when a terrific yellow flame with a heavy and very dense mass of black smoke showed ahead, and the Queen Mary herself was no longer visible. The Tiger was steaming at 24 knots only 500 yards astern of Queen Mary, and hauled sharply out of the line to port and disappeared in this dense mass of smoke. We hauled out to starboard, and Tiger and ourselves passed one on each side of the Queen Mary. We passed her about 50 yards on our port beam by which time the smoke had blown fairly clear, revealing the stern from the after funnel aft afloat, and the propellers still revolving, but the for'ard part had already gone under. There was no sign of fire or of cordite flame, and men were crawling out of the top of the after turret and up the after hatchway. When we were abreast and only about 150 yards away from her, this after portion rolled over and, as it did so, blew up. The most noticeable thing was the masses and masses of paper which were blown into the air as this after portion exploded. Great masses of iron were thrown into the air, and I saw, I suppose at least 100 or 200 feet high, a boat which may have been a dinghy or a pinnace, still intact but upside down as I could

see the thwarts. Before we had quite passed, Queen Mary completely disappeared."

Fifty-seven officers, including Thomas Field, and 1,209 men were killed; two officers and five men wounded. One officer and one man were subsequently rescued by German destroyers. Together with the rest of the crew, Thomas' name appears on the Plymouth Naval Memorial at Southsea.

The Admiralty Roll of Naval Medals and Awards (ADM 171/89) shows that this sixteen year-old received the Victory and War Medals, forwarded to his father after the war.

Thomas is also remembered on the door of St John's Church in Boldre in the New Forest. His grandfather was buried here in 1869 and, some time later, in 1938, Sir Mostyn Field gave new doors to the Church and included on each a memorial respectively to his father and his son. That on the left door reads "In loving memory of John Bousquet Field Captain Royal Navy and of Cecilia his wife at rest in this churchyard also of their grandson" and on the right door "Thomas Mostyn Field aged 16 years Midshipman HMS Queen Mary sunk at Battle of Jutland 31 May 1916 the only son of Admiral Sir Mostyn Field K.C.B. F.R.S. and Lady Field".

Andrew Keeling

References:

1. Winston Churchill, First Lord of the Admiralty, 16 November 1914 (Notes to War Letters Vol. 2).
2. Snotty – naval slang for midshipman.
3. As from HMS Queen Mary, 27th May 1916 in War Letters 1914–1918 Vol. 2: Philip Malet de Carteret, Amazon Kindle Edition, ASIN: B00JOBTMAK, 2014.
4. "Naval Operations" by Sir Julian S. Corbett. Volume III. [History of the Great War based on Official Documents, by direction of the Historical Section of the Committee of Imperial Defence.] (London and New York: Longmans, Green, and Company. 1923.

Geo William Hadley

Lance Corporal George William Hadley Hampshire Regiment (July 1891- 15 September 1916)

George William Hadley was born in July 1891 at Hall Court, Shedfield, Hampshire, where his father was a cab driver, presumably for the Rev. A. Murray-Aynsley, the then owner of what is described in a history of the time as a 'fine country estate'. Hall Court, which has early 18th century origins, has now been converted into five flats but its importance as a building is still recognised through its current Grade II listing.

George was the second of eight children and from the 1901 census clearly spent most of his early childhood at Hall Court. He is next recorded in the 1911 census, when he was 20, working as a domestic groom in Ledbury and living with two widows as a lodger.

By this date, George's mother Emily had also been widowed and was living with five of her sons and her daughter at Hillside, School Rd, Twyford where she remained until her death, a year after George's, in August 1917.

George never married and it appears that, at some time between 1911 and 1915, he returned to Hampshire, probably to Farlington, as we next hear of him volunteering to 'fight the Hun' as part of the Portsmouth Pals in April 1915. It is well known that many northern towns formed Pals battalions during the war but they were not common in the South. The Portsmouth Pals recruited their ranks from men entering Frogmore Road on their way to watch Portsmouth Football Club. They joined the 14th and, in George's case, 15th Battalions Hampshire Regiment. George would no doubt have been influenced by the posters outside the Pompey football ground which read:

> *"Tonight midnight - the final hour for single men. The hands of time are sinking fast, don't sink into the army, come in as a man. Join at once Portsmouth's own."*

After initial training close to home, 15th Battalion joined the 122nd Brigade, 41st Division, at Aldershot in October. Following final training George and his battalion proceeded to France in early May 1916.

There then followed a period of relative inactivity until 14 September, when the battalion moved to the forward trenches at Delville to participate in their first major action, the Battle of Flers-Courcelette, between 15-22 September. This was the third main phase of the Battle of the Somme. It is best known as the first tank battle in history. All 49 tanks that the British army possessed were deployed. However 17 of them failed to reach the front line and a further seven failed to work at zero hour. Churchill, who had championed the development of the tank complained, *"my poor 'land battleships' have been let off prematurely on a petty scale".'*

George, who by this date, perhaps because at 25 he was a bit more mature than most of his fellow soldiers, had been promoted to lance corporal and would no doubt have led his men 'over the top' and been more exposed to enemy fire than many. The 41st Division, of which he was part, had the job of capturing Flers and was given the most tanks. The village was captured early on but unfortunately George was killed, probably en route, close to Delville Wood.

It is interesting to refer to the 15th Battalion war diary to get a feel for what it must have been like for George at the front, experiencing such intense action for the first time:

> *Place: Fricourt*
>
> *11th Sept. 3.15am Battalion marched to Fricourt. Arrived 5.50 am*
>
> *12th Sept. 3.00am Battalion moved to trenches as reserve to 164th 6.00pm Battalion returned to camp near Fricourt.*
>
> *Place: Trenches W. of Delville Wood*
>
> *13th Sept. 6.15 pm Batt. relieves 20th D.L.I. Relief complete by 6.15 am.*
>
> *14th Sept. Our artillery very active all day shelling Flers and Bapaume.*
>
> *11.00pm Moved to Assembly Trenches. Two platoon commanders killed.*
>
> *Place: Attack*
>
> *15th Sept. 6.20 am Action commenced with the Batt. moving across no-man's-land, just behind the barrage. The barrage was excellent – just what the men had been trained to expect – and came up to expectations so far as keeping the enemy quiet. Things were not so satisfactory on our left, however, for a full ten minutes were taken up before the machine guns were silenced. These guns took heavy toll of the left platoon. Of company commanders – no less than three were fatally hit before the first objective was won. One of these guns was put out by two men who walked along the trench and shot the team.*

The second objective was taken with less trouble, many of the enemy running towards Flers without equipment or arms. The armoured 'cars' did not, up to this point, do much except perhaps cause alarm in the second enemy line, owing to their having dropped behind.

The Batt., with the 12th batt. on our right and the 18th K.R.R.C. on our left, swept on to Flers which was entered, more or less cleared and passed. It was during this period that one of the armoured 'cars' did most useful work smashing one of the enemy strong points and without doubt demoralising them. It also gave the men great confidence.

Meanwhile losses had been fairly heavy owing to the heavy barrage put up by the Germans.

In the following week the offensive got bogged down, partly because of heavy rain, and failed to achieve its main aim of punching a hole in the German lines.

The war diary records that during this battle, 15th Battalion casualties comprised eight officers killed and five wounded and 31 other ranks killed, 60 missing and 188 wounded. This was a huge proportion of the 550 or so that made up the battalion.

George's body was never recovered and he is commemorated on the nearby Thiepval War Memorial along with the many others who died in this battle.

George was one of those remembered in a special memorial service for the fallen held on 5 November at Twyford Church.

In the UK, George is commemorated, not only on the Twyford War Memorial but also on the First World War Cross at Farlington, and more recently on a memorial plaque at Fratton Park; installed in 2014 to commemorate all the Portsmouth Pals who served in the First World War particularly the 1,400 who were killed.

Four of George's brothers also served during the war but fortunately survived and are remembered for their service on the Twyford Village Hall commemorative plaque.

Jeff Mardon

Editor's Note:
The losses experienced by the battalion mentioned above are somewhat different from those recorded in the Hampshire Chronicle article on Walter Cox, also in the 15th Battalion and who took part in same battle. The figures above are extracted from the Battalion's War Diary (WO 95/2632/2 &/3) and so

reflect the position at the time, those in the Cox article may have been prepared subsequently and included some revision. Either way the figures are dreadful.

The Thiepval Memorial, designed by Sir Edwin Lutyens, commemorates more than 72,000 men of British and South African forces who have no known grave, the majority of whom died during the Somme offensive of 1916.

Walter Chas C Cox

Private Walter Charles Clavey Cox Hampshire Regiment (15 August 1900 – 7 October 1916)

When trawling through the Church filing cabinet a few years ago, I came across a couple of Hampshire Chronicle articles about Boy Soldier Walter Cox. Dating from 2004, they recorded how a Mr Richard Fowler of Horncastle, Lincolnshire had been trying to find out about his late father's cousin, Walter Charles Clavey Cox. He had contacted the Chronicle to determine whether he was commemorated on a War Memorial in Hampshire and, if so, which one. In a remarkably short time he was put in touch with several Hampshire folk (including Stanley Crooks, Sue Sullivan, Mark Bailey, Joan Freemantle and Steve Jarvis) and one result of this was a very full article several weeks later in the Chronicle entitled "Walter uncovered". Really so much was covered by Mr Fowler and the Chronicle that I don't think I can do better than quote much of these two articles verbatim (some selection and slight re-ordering has been made).

"Walter Charles Clavey Cox was barely sixteen years old when he lost his life in the First World War. He has no known grave and is commemorated on the Thiepval Memorial, France, along with 72,000 comrades.

"He enlisted in Winchester and was recorded at the time as resident in Twyford. His movements can be traced through his Regiment and Battalion. He belonged to the 15th Battalion Hampshire Regiment, all of whom were volunteers. It was one of the so-called New Army units allocated to the 41st Division. The battalion had spent most of 1915 at Portsmouth, and moved first to Witley in Surrey and then into barracks at Aldershot.

"The men arrived in France in May 1916, and went first to Meteren and then to 'Plugstreet Wood'[1], where they had their first taste of trench warfare - and suffered their first casualties.

"After being subject to gas attacks and enemy raids, the 15th were moved from Plugstreet to the Somme for the big offensives planned for 15 September 1916. The battalion distinguished itself that day helping to recapture the town of Flers, where today a fine memorial to the men of the 41st Division stands. But the battle had taken its toll of the 15th Hampshires – of the 18 officers and 557 men, eight officers and 97 men were killed, and three officers and 197 men were wounded.

Walter Cox, from Miss Hull's Photo Album

"Walter survived that day – the 15th's first battle – and he would have been witness to the sight of the British secret weapon, the tank, being deployed for the first time in modern warfare. But he was to lose his life less than a month later, Walter was killed in action on 7 October 1916, during an attack on Gird Trench and Gird Support north-east of Eaucourt, Somme.

"His obituary appeared in the Hampshire Chronicle in early November 1916: Twyford: Killed in Action - We regret to announce the death of Pte Walter C. C. Cox of 3, The Drove, Twyford, who was killed in action on the 7th inst. The deceased, who was only 16 years of age on the 15th August last, joined up as of the age of 18, and was 5 feet 10½ inches in height[2]. He enlisted for seven years in the Regulars, and nothing could be done to restrain him from doing his duty, and to fight for his country and friends. The deceased was a member of the Church Lads' Brigade, under Col. Yorke for about three years, and member of the Twyford Bible Class. He leaves a widowed mother and young brother and sister to mourn his loss. Deceased was much liked in the village, being very popular, happy and bright.

"The Twyford Bible Class mentioned in the obituary was held by Miss Leila Hull, from 1913, and written about in Stanley Crooks' *'Twyford 20th Century Chronicle'* published in 2000.

"Mr Crooks describes what happened when war broke out: 'They (the boys from our village who went to her Bible Class) wrote to her from many parts of the world, and sent photos of themselves in uniform. She wrote to all of them and remembered them in her prayers. Miss Hull started her scrapbook, putting in pictures of all her boys ... against some she wrote a sad RIP – for Private Walter Cox, for Peter Barnard, for Jack Powell, aged eighteen, for Frank Dumper who died in India. For Fred Cox[3], who died aged seventeen after a long illness.'

"Sadly Mr Fowler was to find out later that the Fred Cox mentioned in the text, was Walter's younger brother, Frederick Harold Jack Cox, born 1909.

He further discovered that "... his great-uncle Walter Cox married Blanche Lotten in Droxford in 1899. They had three children. Boy soldier Walter was the eldest, and Fred the youngest. Between them came Blanche Emily Cox, born 1903. She died unmarried, in June 1928, and both she and Fred are buried in St Mary's Churchyard, Twyford. So ended the other part of Mr Fowler's quest – to trace any descendants of Walter's younger brother and sister.

"Stanley Crooks' book *'Ringing the Changes'*, also referred to 'old Mrs Cox' who enjoyed a glass of Guinness at the Dolphin Inn," said Mr Fowler. "Joan Freemantle spoke to some 90-plus-year-olds who confirmed that this was indeed Walter's mother, who lived at Dolphin Cottage. Poor woman, by the age of 50 she had lost her husband and all three children."[4]

With the benefit of the more recent availability of some documents, there are a few further snippets we can add.

In 1901 the family were living in Petersfield, at 33 High Street. Walter senior was 22, Blanche 30 and Walter junior was just eight months (confirming his birth date of August the previous year). They were both working for Mr Francis Townley, the proprietor of The Dolphin Hotel, and living there as well. Walter senior's job jumped out at me as I hadn't seen the word for so long. He was the ostler.[5] Walter junior's birthplace is recorded as Botley, Hampshire.

Ten years later they were still over at Petersfield, but Walter senior was the Coachman, at Fair Oak Lodge in Rogate. Blanche was working as a dressmaker and Walter, aged ten, was at school. Blanche junior was aged eight and Frederick three. They also had living with them Blanche's nephew, Horace Welch. He was 25, single and working as a Domestic Gardener.

We can see from the Medals Index that Walter was approved for receipt of the British War Medal and the Victory Medal in May 1920. These would have gone to Blanche doubtless some years after that, a long wait.

Christopher Pope.

Notes:

1. Plugstreet – the Tommies' name for the Walloon village of Ploegsteert, in Belgium, 15 km south of Ypres and just over the border from Armentieres.
2. The Parish Magazine for February 1916 records Walter as already enlisted in the Hampshire Regiment, when he would have been 15.
3. Fred (Frederick Harold Jack) Cox was 3 in 1911 and so too young to serve in the war. He died on 13 January 1926.
4. The Hampshire Chronicle, Friday 22 October 2004, page 10 and Hampshire Chronicle, Friday 24 December 2004, 'Walter uncovered'.
5. Ostler - A man employed to look after the horses of people staying at an inn.

The Dolphin Inn, circa 1914

Edwin Platt

Captain Edwin Platt 8th Canadian Battalion, 90th Winnipeg Rifles (14 February 1892 - 11 April 1917)

Edwin Platt was not a Twyford man by birth or residence, he became one by marriage: he was born on 14 February 1892 in Dorchester, the son of Thomas and Alice Platt. The 1901 census finds the Platt family at 8 Mareden Terrace, Culliford Road, Dorchester. Thomas Platt was a Wine Merchants Foreman, then aged 42 and born in Mexborough, Yorkshire. His wife Alice, also 42, was born in Doncaster. Edwin, then nine years old, had four elder siblings, all born in Yorkshire, and a younger sister.

By 1911 Edwin had moved to Norwich where he was working as a carpet salesman in a furnishing warehouse. The 1911 census also provides the clue why Edwin moved to Canada. By that year his parents Thomas and Alice had moved to Wales and were living in Monmouthshire, Thomas working as a Wine Merchants Cellarman. In the household was son Arthur, a carpenter aged 25 and a Canadian citizen. He had emigrated in 1907 and the 1911 Canadian Census reports him as a lodger at 111 Osborne Street, Winnipeg. Two years later Edwin himself moved to Canada, sailing from Southampton on the Cunard Line's SS Ausonia, which docked at Quebec on 9 June 1913. He proceeded to Winnipeg where he proposed to find work as a salesman.

After the outbreak of the war in August 1914 Edwin was an early volunteer, joining the Canadian Expeditionary Force, 8th Winnipeg Rifles which formed part of the 2nd Canadian Infantry Brigade of the First Canadian Division. He arrived at Valcartier near Quebec in early September 1914 for enlistment. He joined as a private soldier, 5ft 8ins tall with fair hair and blue eyes. Distinguishing marks described as 'small scar on right forefinger and hairy mole on chest'. On his Attestation Papers[1] he gave his next of kin as his mother, Mrs A Platt of 81 Dale Street, Scunthorpe. (His father Thomas Hudson Platt had died in 1913, aged 54, still living and presumably working in Wales.)

The early conditions at Valcartier were basic and much time was spent on preparing accommodation, equipment, training and preparation for war. (Eventually the camp held over 35,000 troops). Edwin was among the first to leave for England, sailing on SS Franconia on 3 October 1914. The voyage took about 12 days and the convoy was escorted by British warships. Since German submarines were reported in the English Channel, the convoy docked at Plymouth instead of Southampton[2], proceeding by train to Salisbury Plain. Here, after a fine autumn, come the end of October the weather turned: steady rain provided very unpleasant conditions. No permanent accommodation was available for the Canadians. A programme of building huts began, but was much hampered by the appalling weather. By December the 2nd and 3rd Infantry Brigades had moved into huts in Larkhill. Training continued, but, recognising the dip in morale with the appalling conditions, six days leave was granted before Christmas to all ranks with a free rail ticket to anywhere in the British Isles. Perhaps Edwin went to visit his mother in Scunthorpe and his siblings. It is improbable that he had met his future wife, Edith Stone.

Soldiers of the 8th Battalion, 90th Winnipeg Rifles attending the Divine Service at Stonehenge, 1915, © IWM (Q 53602)

Returning to Salisbury Plain and further training, after a review by King George V and Lord Kitchener, the main body of Canadian troops embarked from Avonmouth for Saint-Nazaire in France in February 1915, disembarking on 13 February. The West Country port was chosen once again because of the threat from submarines. Upon arrival the Canadian troops proceeded to the Western Front, where they were inspected and favourably commented upon by Sir John French, Commander-in-Chief of the British Expeditionary Force. Then, divided into brigade groups, they joined British divisions for training in trench warfare before serving on the Western

Front. An early engagement for the 8th Winnipeg Rifles was on 14 March at Neuve-Chapelle. They subsequently fought on the Ypres Salient, living up to their nickname 'The Little Black Devils'. The battalion was in action again at Festubert during the war in the trenches. They also fought in the Battle of the Somme (June 1915-June 1916)[3]. On 10 May 1915 Edwin was granted a temporary commission as a lieutenant, and later that year he went on a machine gun course from which he returned on 25 September 1915. In November 1915 he had a week's leave (though it is not clear if this was in England).

It was during the first months of 1916 that Edwin married Edith Stone, daughter of John Thomas Stone, Engineer at the Waterworks in Twyford. Thus began his association with the village, though it is unclear how they met. No evidence is gained from Hazeley Down Camp records and only general information in the Hampshire Chronicle of Canadian soldiers attending church parades and social functions in Twyford Parish Hall in 1916. There is no such information in 1915. In February 1916 he again had leave in England and was promoted to Captain. The marriage took place on 12 February 1916 at St Peter's Church, Onslow Square, Kensington by licence. Edwin was then 23 and the address he gave was 190 Kildonan Avenue, Kildonan, Winnipeg. Edith was also 23 and gave her address as 123 Queensgate, SW. His leave was extended to 4 March 1916. He had a further seven days' leave in May.

On 23 September 1916 Edwin was attached for duty with the Director of Graves Registration Committee. In March 1917 he was posted to the Motor Machine Gun Brigade: this was probably during the careful and detailed planning for the attack on Vimy Ridge, in which the Canadians played a prominent and famous role. From 24 March the Ridge was under constant shelling from Canadian and British batteries. It was during this battle that Edwin was killed by an enemy shell near Thelus. The circumstances of casualty read:

> *"Killed in Action (11 April 1917)*
> *While on duty in the Trenches North West of Thelus he was instantly killed by an enemy shell burst close to him".*

Edwin Platt was buried in the Ecoivres Military Cemetery at Mont St Eloi, five km north-west of Arras. He was 25.

Before this battle, as was often the case, Edwin wrote a touching letter to his father-in-law, John Stone, asking him to take the necessary steps in the event of his death:

Dear Dad

Should you be advised that it is necessary to act upon this. Please get in touch with A Platt, 190 Kildonan Av W Kildonan. W peg Canada & the Bank of Montreal. They have my monies in their care. Also make enquiries & take steps to see that pension is laid down in Can: Orders of approx. $400 per year is paid to Edith. Your letter regarding this should be addressed to the Can: Pay & Records Office Millbank London S.W. Be of good cheer all is well. I am, but I write to you thus that there may be no confusion, & unnecessary worry to my Girlie. I know you will do this, Edith is my all in life & my thoughts are of her always.

For the rest I am here to lick the hun.

Cheer Oh Boy Ted.

Back in Twyford the following appeared in Twyford Parish Magazine for May 1917.

It is with very great sorrow that I have heard of the death of Captain E Platt, of the 1st Canadian Contingent at the Front. Our deepest sympathy goes out to his young widow, and to Mr and Mrs Stone. In such a grievous time as this words seem very hard to find and very worthless, as these brave and gallant soldiers give up their lives for others.

Now the labourer's task is o'er';
Now the battle day is past;
Now upon the farther shore
Lands the voyager at last.
Father in Thy gracious keeping
Leave we now Thy servant sleeping.
H S Morris (Vicar)

Edwin's medals and decorations, the 14/15 Star, the Plaque and Scroll, and the Memorial Cross were sent to Edith Platt. Edith Platt continued to live at the Waterworks. In February 1920 she and her father each gave £5 towards the Twyford War Memorial which was erected in the Church on 4 April 1920. In 1924 she was Leader of the Scouts in Twyford ('Ringing the Changes', a Twyford publication). On New Year's Day 1930 in Twyford Church Edith Platt married again: her husband was Peter John Campbell Thomson, a bachelor and a retired Master Mariner who lived in Bromley, Kent.

Sue Kennedy

References and Notes:

1. Service File RG 150 Accession 1992 – 93/166 Box 7862 – 50 Library and Archives of Canada.
2. A prudent precaution, the U-boat threat was real. The Franconia survived only two years from Edwin's voyage. On 4 October 1916, still employed as an auxiliary transport, the Cunarder was en route from Alexandria to Marseille, when she was torpedoed and sunk by the German submarine UB-47 (Kaptlt. Wolfgang Steinbauer). Fortunately she was not carrying troops. Of her crew of 314, twelve were killed and 302 rescued by the hospital ship HMHS Dover Castle. The Wreck Site: https://www.wrecksite.eu/wreck.aspx?13709. The Ausonia, suffered the same fate, on 30 May 1918, on passage from Montreal to Avonmouth with general cargo, she was sunk by the German submarine U-62 (Ernst Hashagen), 620 miles WxS3/4S from Fastnet. 44 persons were lost. The Wreck Site: https://www.wrecksite.eu/wreck.aspx?13708.
3. Canadian Expeditionary Force, 1914-1919: Official History of the Canadian Army in the First World War by G.W.L. Nicholson (Queen's Printer, Ottawa, 1962), ISBN: 978-0773546172, on line at www.cmp-cpm.forces.gc.ca/dhh-dhp/his/oh-ho/index-eng.asp.

Twyford Waterworks early in the 20th Century. The house of John Stone, the Engineer and Manager, and father of Edith, is in the background on the left

George Mansell

Private George Mansell Dorsetshire Regiment (1886 - 15 April 1917)

The Mansells are a long-established local family. A count of the occurrence of the family name in the parish registers between 1837 and the late 1920s, comes up with no less than 87 entries. Several Mansells went off to the war, including Frederick, George and George Harry. George was not to return and Harry came back wounded. Readers who may have known Harry, for many years Captain of Bells at St Mary's, and indeed his son Roy, currently living in Shipley Road, may like to know that the Georges were first cousins, sharing grandparents George senior and Ellen, mentioned later in this story.

George was born in 1886. His parents, James and Isabella had been married in St Mary's Church on 20 November 1882, when the building was brand new, its consecration just four years before. The groom was 26 and a baker, and the bride was 27.

George was the third of their children. James Frederick was two years older and Ellen Elizabeth, born in 1885, was sadly to die 11 months later while Isabella was very pregnant with George; a cruel blow. George was named after his paternal grandfather and was baptised at St Mary's on the 28 March 1886. But there was further tragedy in store for this young family when, the following year, both James and Isabella died. Isabella was buried at St Mary's on 20 February, there is no record at St Mary's of James' death.

So George went to live with his grandparents George and Ellen Mansell. A little while later, in 1901, George and Ellen, 72 and 62 respectively, were providing a home on the High Street for one of their daughters, four grandchildren and two boarders. George junior was 15 and working as a Bricklayers Labourer.

In September 1910 George married. His bride was Annie Eliza Hewitt and they must have been married in her parish, there being no entry for the event in our records. Their first home was in the High Street in Twyford where they started their family with baby Daisy Drusilla arriving later that year. She was baptised on 4 December but sadly died very shortly afterwards. George continued to work locally as a gardener and as a Stoker at the Waterworks on the Hazeley Road.

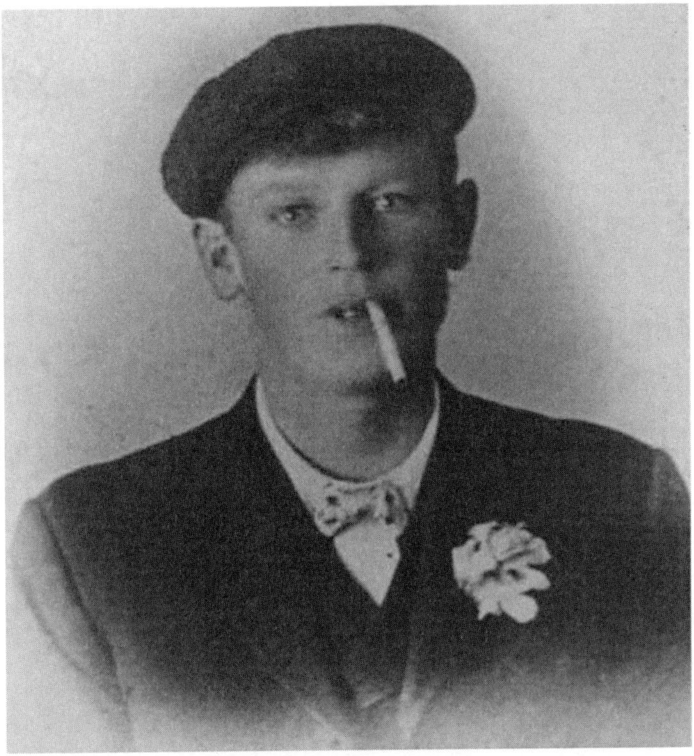

George Mansell

We can actually see George's workplace there today, thanks to the restoration of the site by the Twyford Waterworks Trust. George's job would have involved loading the coal outside in the yard into small trucks on a two foot gauge railway and pushing these to the weighbridge and then along the lines into the Boiler House, emptying them onto the floor and then shovelling the coal into the furnaces of the Babcock and Wilcox boilers that were the latest technology being installed at that time. For efficient operation the correct amounts of coal had to be supplied at just the right time. George would have had to climb the ladder to the top of the boiler to check the pressure gauges there and adjust the water levels in the boiler. The steam produced drove the various engines and pumps at the plant, for raising the water from the wells, distributing it within the premises and finally up to the reservoirs on the down (up Watley Lane), for supply to the village. It was a three-shift operation with six men on a shift and the largest employer in the village. [At the works George would have known Edith Stone, daughter of John Thomas Stone, the Engineer and Manager there, who would later marry Edwin Platt. Edwin is also commemorated on our war memorial.]

The Babcock and Wilcox boilers at Twyford Waterworks that George tended

In due course another baby arrived, William James, born in early 1913 and baptised at St Mary's on 12 January.

Following the outbreak of war George was keen to join up and headed for the Hampshire Regiment, he must have been 28. From his regimental number, 2644, we deduce that he joined in September 1914. The Parish Magazine records him in January and August 1915 as serving in the National Reserve. In January 1916 another record places him in the 5th Battalion, this would be the 3/5th formed at Southampton in March 1915 as a "third line" unit, ie Territorial Force unit, intended for service in the UK. It moved to Bournemouth later in the year and on 8 April 1916 was renamed 5th Reserve Battalion and based at Romsey.[1]

So for much of 1915 and 1916 George was in the UK and not very far from home. He would have had time off and hopefully been able to enjoy the arrival of his third child, Florence May, at the end of 1915. Florence was christened on 23 January 1916[2]. [She spent much of her life in Twyford and is remembered living in School Road after the Second World War].

By 1916 it was clear that the war would not be won by volunteers alone and the Military Service Acts, January and May, brought in conscription. These also made provisions, contrary to the Territorial and Reserve Forces Act of 1907, that a man serving in a Territorial corps could, without his consent, be transferred to another corps or to the regular army or to any unit within the same corps. This would explain how, early in 1917, George was transferred to the 1st Battalion of the Dorsetshire Regiment. From his new regimental number, 19683, this occurred on/about the 17 January.

From there on things moved rapidly for George. His new battalion had been engaged in France since August 1914 and had been in and out of action. It was now part of the 14th Infantry Brigade, in the 32nd Division. The battalion had been in action at Mons and Pont Fixe in 1914, at Ypres and on 5 May 1915 at Hill 60 it was the first British unit to face a gas attack. In 1916 it had been heavily engaged in the Battle of the Somme suffering substantial losses.

George probably arrived at his new unit in late January or February of 1917. He would have come in with a draft of replacements arriving to bring the battalion up to strength and build up the army in France and Flanders. (Between 1 January and 1 August 1917 the size of the army grew from 1,591,745 to 2,044,627 men. [3])

When George arrived the brigade was in the line in the valley of the river Ancre. The valley had degenerated into the devastated landscape which we identify with the Western Front. Dudley Ward describes aspects of the scene that would have greeted George:

> *"... the physical effort required to reach the front line was enormous. Men would slip from the boards and sink up to their knees in a tenacious quality of soft mud; the long gum boots, which reached to the thigh, were wrenched from them; all movement was an exhaustive struggle. Trenches remained in name only, a convenient reference to a locality; actually troops were dotted about in small, shell-hole posts."*[4]

However their deployment was to change. Towards the end of February the 32nd Division was moved to the southern end of the British line, arriving at Le Quesnil on the 24th where they took over a sector on the Amiens-Roye road (now the D934), about 85 km from St Quentin. The area was generally quiet.

Earlier, in 1916, the German High Command had come to a decision about the front line in this area, resolving to shorten it. Enormous resources had been deployed to build a highly fortified series of defences that came to be known as 'The Hindenberg Line', some 90 miles long, at points up to 20 miles behind the present line. In the middle of March the Germans started a very carefully planned and controlled withdrawal to this line.

The allied forces facing them were now involved in a new kind of "semi-open" warfare, seeking to exploit the German retreat and having to deal with the bombs, booby traps and scorched earth tactics that the enemy had deployed as they left. The situation was fluid and there were plenty of Germans in strong positions delaying the allied advance. The Dorsets were involved in these delicate movements that needed to be co-ordinated with the French troops on their right, with nobody sure at what point they would find the Germans dug in for determined resistance. Many of these attacks were at one- or two-company level, rather than the set piece multi-battalion advances that we associate with the Western Front.

From 18 March the battalion had been involved in this general advance, which would have involved George in a lot of marching and hard work repairing the infrastructure destroyed by the Germans, building bridges and filling in craters in the roads. In the course of 7 April they were relieved by 11th Border Regiment and "went back to Germaine where baths were available" and four days of rest and respite.

But the brigade was soon called back to continue the advance. On 12/13 April the Dorsets had patrols out near St Quentin and on the 14th one of these attacks involved the taking of Cepy Farm. It was a "rushed" action in response to an unexpected order. At 6.30 am Captain Hands of C Company was ordered to take the farm, we suspect George was in this company. The attack went in at 7.30 am and by 9.00 am the farm was in their hands. Ward quotes an eye witness report (D. Stayner) that:

> *"The attack went forward in extended line with great dash ... One saw men dropping here and there but it did not cause any wavering in the advance, across about six hundred yards of open ground. It was magnificent to watch ... ".*[5]

The War Diary estimated that the defenders amounted to "at least half a company", and they were observed running away before C Company arrived, even so seven prisoners were taken.[6]

But the German tactics were clearly well planned and the attackers were not in position long before an intense artillery bombardment started, together with concerted machine gun fire from St Quentin. This continued throughout the day and the following night. On the 15th ...

> *"Cepy Farm was subjected to a very heavy bombardment throughout the day which grew in intensity towards the evening ... The garrison of the farm suffered heavily. The casualties were (two second lieutenants) and 13 other ranks (O.R.s) killed, a further 4 officers and 22 O.R.s wounded.* [7]

That evening the battalion handed over to companies of the 5/6th Royal Scots and 15th HLI, the relief being completed at 6.30 am on the 16th.

The War Graves Commission records 15 April as the date of George's death. This indicates that he had been involved in that stirring attack on the farm the previous day and was one of the 15 killed in the artillery bombardment the day after.

The War Diary contains two letters of congratulation for the battalion, both dated the 17th, from the generals commanding 14th Brigade and 32nd Division, for the "dash" and "tenacity" displayed in the Cepy Farm attack, that from the Divisional Commander, Major General Cameron D. Shute, expressing his distress at the heavy losses incurred from shellfire. This latter is handwritten. On the 30th he visited the battalion to inspect it and hand out 'gongs'.

The battalion was then out of the front line until 18 June, involved in training and general recuperation.

George's death was announced in the Parish Magazine in June 1917 with the Rev H.S. Morris expressing his deepest sympathy to Annie and their young children. Some time after the war Annie would have received George's medals, the British War Medal and the Victory Medal and in November 1919 she received the balance of George's monies from the War Office, consisting of his final pay plus a gratuity, a total of £17/14/10 (current day value, approx. £620). She died in Twyford in 1952.

George has no known grave. He is commemorated on the Thiepval memorial, on Pier 7 and Face B, about 40 km to the north and west of where he was killed.

Barbara Mansell
Christopher Pope

References:

1. 1/5th Battalion sailed for India on 9 October 1914, landing at Karachi 11 November and remaining in India for the rest of the war and the 2/5th Battalion, formed on Salisbury Plain in September 1914 as a home service ("second line") unit although also being sent to India on 13 December 1914. Ref: The Long, Long Trail - http://www.longlongtrail.co.uk/army/regiments-and-corps/the-british-infantry-regiments-of-1914-1918/hampshire-regiment/.
2. St Mary's Parish Registers (Baptisms) (http://www.tomccparishes.org.uk/wp-content/uploads/2015/04/Twyford-Baptisms-1838-to-1920-revised-7-July-2008.pdf) and family records.
3. History of the Dorsetshire Regiment 1914-1919, Part 1 The Regular Battalions by Major C.H. Dudley Ward DSO, MC, pub. Henry Ling Ltd., Dorchester, page 97.
4. Ward, page 98.
5. Ward, page 105.
6. War Diary, 1st Battalion Devonshire Regiment, The National Archives, ref WO-95-2392/1-2, sheet 91.
7. War Diary, sheet 93.

From the Twyford Womens Institute Scrapbook, 1917, members mending shoes, illustrating how the village managed with the men away, Miss Pavey, Mrs Meath, Mrs Foard, Mrs Hickman and Mrs Stubbington (County Records Office 26M89/16)

Walter Shave

Private Frederick Walter Shave Worcestershire Regiment (1883 – 1 June 1917)

Frederick Walter Shave's connection with Twyford has proved somewhat tenuous.

He was born in 1883 in Lytchett Matravers, near Poole in Dorset, the second son of Alfred Shave and his wife Ann. His elder brother Archibald's birth had been registered in Poole during the winter of the previous year. By 1891 the family was living at Morley Cottage in Winfrith Newburgh near Wareham, along with his younger brother Robert James (then four, born in Whitchurch) and sister Edith Mary (baptised 9 June 1889 in Wool); his father was then working as a gamekeeper. By 1901, when Walter was about 18, the family had moved to Ampfield in Hampshire, where Walter was working as a carter on a farm as was his brother Robert; Archibald was working as an agricultural labourer, and two younger brothers had been born whilst the family were at Winfrith: Frank born around 1893 and William Samuel born during the winter of 1895 and baptised on 14 July 1895.

During the winter of 1907 Walter, aged about 24, married Caroline Edith Lepper. Caroline was aged about 18, and had been born in Maidstone, the fourth child of George Lepper and his wife Hannah. They were married at St Nicholas and Good Shepherd, Wisley with Pyrford near Guildford. By 1911 Walter and Caroline were living at Coombe, East Meon, and had three daughters born in rapid succession: Edith, born in 1909 at Pyrford, Florence born in 1910 in Chalton in Middlesex, and Esther, born in 1911 at Southwick, Hampshire. Walter was described as a wagoner which may account for the family's frequent moves.

By this time the rest of the family had moved again, now closer to Twyford, and were living at Hazeley in Morestead – his father was still working as a gamekeeper and brother Archie still a farm labourer; Robert and Frank were also working as wagoners, and William was another farm labourer. There is no mention of Walter's sister Edith; so far I have failed to find any record of her marriage or death, but a Miss Edith Shave from Harebreaks in Walford did emigrate to Australia on 6 September 1923 aged 33 and it's just possible this is her. The family does include four year old Ruby Shave, a grand-daughter born in Woking in 1907. So far I have been unable to find further details of Ruby; Walter's brothers all appear to be unmarried but Ruby's surname is given as Shave: was she perhaps Edith's daughter living with her grandparents and taking their surname after her mother's early death, or the illegitimate daughter of Edith or of one of Walter's unmarried brothers, or the daughter of Edith and a Shave cousin who was just visiting her grandparents?

By 1917, with the country at war, Walter had joined the Worcestershire Regiment (Private 36495). His military records are very scanty and I have been unable to discover when he joined up; he served first with the 4th Battalion, was then transferred to the 10th Battalion, and then back to the 4th Battalion with whom he was serving when he died.[1] If he had not already enlisted, he would have been conscripted in May 1916, when he was 33 and when conscription for those aged 18-41 was extended to married men.

His military service would have been wrapped up in the activities of those two Worcestershire battalions with which we believe he was involved.

The 4th Battalion served at Gallipoli in 1915, and then in France, landing in Marseille on 20 March 1916. During the summer of 1916 they fought on the Somme, at Ypres and then in the Somme again on The Transloy Ridges, where conditions were made even worse by atrocious weather. By the spring of 1917 they were involved in the Battle of Arras (9 April - 16 May). On 23-24 April the battalion attacked at the head of the 88th Brigade (29th Division) in the Second Battle of the Scarpe, capturing three lines of German trenches.

The 10th Battalion was raised in September 1914 and left for France in July 1915. During the winter of 1916 they were in the trenches at Neuve Chapelle; in April 1916 they were withdrawn into General Reserve for training which continued until June when they fought on the Somme. In July 1916 they participated in the successful storming of La Boiselle, in the course of which both the colonel and his adjutant were killed in quick succession; this was one of the first occasions when some officers had been deliberately left behind before an attack in order to replace inevitable casualties. By mid-May 1917 the battalion was involved in the preparations for the Battle of Messines.

Walter died on 1 June 1917. As he was not killed in action, but died of wounds, it is not possible to be sure exactly when he was wounded or in which operation this occurred. The 4th Battalion's war diary however gives a vivid picture of the last months of Walter's life which involved impromptu skirmishes, fierce fighting in a set-piece advance and a lot of marching, numerous Church parades, training and the occasional bath. During this period men were killed and wounded not only in the skirmishes and attack, but also in their own trenches and on the march.

Towards the end of this period, on 14 May, the battalion was ordered back into reserve trenches outside Arras at Hangest Work. On 16 May they relieved the 6th Battalion which had been reduced to fewer than 200 men; the next day their lines were shelled and two men were wounded. On 18 May they improved their trenches and supplied fatigue parties to brigade and on the night of 20/21 May they were relieved and in turn relieved others in the front line. On 22 May an officer and two men were wounded trying to establish one of four advance posts in front of the front line, before the position was found to be untenable and the attempt abandoned. They were relieved again on 24 May, and spent the next five days at Railway Triangle where the time was spent in cleaning equipment, inspecting kit and billets, bathing and musketry practice. On 25 May half of the officers and 10% of the other ranks were allowed a one-hour pass to Arras. On 28 May three men were wounded by shrapnel at Railway Triangle before they returned to the front line that night; on 29 May their trenches were heavily shelled all day, killing ten and wounding a further six. On 30 May there were heavy thunderstorms leaving the battalion above its knees in mud and water in many places. At 11.25 pm they attacked an enemy post, resulting in an extremely heavy German barrage on their trenches making it impossible to advance further; a German counter-attack was repulsed and documents taken from enemy dead revealed that the Germans had planned an attack on their trenches at the same time as the British had attacked the Germans. This last operation cost a further 12 lives with two more missing and 27 wounded. If not wounded earlier, Walter is likely to have been one of these 27, as no men were recorded wounded on 31 May or 1 June.

Walter was buried at Duisans British Cemetery, Etrun in the Pas de Calais (grave IV.M.42), three miles west of Arras. His grave is marked with a cross, engraved with his name and date of death but with no additional text. This was the cemetery for the 8th, 19th and 41st Casualty Clearing Stations, with burials taking place from these stations from March 1917 until April 1918. Walter is one of 3,207 Commonwealth servicemen buried there, along with 88 German war dead – most of them casualties of these Battles of Arras and the trench warfare which followed.

Walter was awarded a British War Medal and a Victory Medal (the latter being issued to most of those awarded a British War Medal, as well as to all those who won a 1914 Star or a 1914-1915 Star). The British War Medal was instituted on 26 July 1919 for those serving between 5 August 1914 and 11 November 1918.

British War Medal

Victory Medal

Although he lived in East Meon at the time of the 1911 census, Walter does not appear on the East Meon war memorial, but as well as appearing on our memorial he is one of 18 First World War names on the roll of honour on the Cheriton War Memorial: perhaps the family had moved here between the 1911 census and his death. Here he is recorded as "Fred W Shave", suggesting that perhaps whilst his parents and siblings knew him as Walter, his wife preferred to call him Fred.

At the age of 30, Caroline was left a widow with three daughters under ten. Two years later, she married again, in St Peter's, Woking on 22 November 1919. Her second husband, and step-father to Walter's three young daughters, was James William Pullen (then aged 36).

Walter's brothers Frank and William Shave joined up early, Frank joining the Coldstream Guards (Private 9292) in August 1914[2], and William the Army Service Corps (Private M/286143) in September 1914, as recorded in the Parish Magazine. Both of them were amongst those named in August 1915 in the discussion about a memorial for those who served in the war. Frank won a 1914 Star (a British Empire Medal nicknamed the Mons Star as most recipients had taken part in the retreat from Mons), approved in 1917 for those who had served at the First Battle of Ypres (between August and midnight on 22/23 November 1914), as well as a British War Medal and a Victory Medal. Like Walter, William won a Victory Medal and a British War Medal. Frank and William do not appear in the Commonwealth War Graves Commission database, so presumably survived the war.

I have found no records of military service for Archibald or Robert, although both would seem to have been liable to conscription. A Robert J Shave, who is presumably Walter's brother, died in Winchester in March 1936, and an Archibald Shave, who may be Walter's older brother, married an Ellen LM Ashdown in late summer 1928 in Southampton, and died in Winchester in 1962; he was buried in Magdalen Hill cemetery on 21 May 1962[3].

Susie Biddle

References:

1. This is based on the details of his previous regiments in the WWI Service Medals and Annual Rolls.
2. His Medal record refers to a disembarkation date of 21 August 1914.
3. Grave Q/55, section D Con, internment number 8480.

Notes:

1. Census for 1891, 1901, 1911 (accessed via www.ancestry.co.uk).
2. National Archives at www.nationalarchives.gov.uk including WO 95/2309/2 War Diary or Intelligence Survey of the 4th Battalion Worcestershire Regiment March 1916 – April 1919.
3. Roll of Honour website at www.roll-of-honour.com/Hampshire/Cheriton.html.

Queen Street, during the war

Walter Chas H Feltham

Sergeant Walter Charles Henry Feltham Hampshire Regiment (13 March 1886 - 4 October 1917)

Walter was born on 13 March 1886 in the little Salisbury Plain village of Chitterne All Saints to a 19 year-old local girl Hannah Feltham, a domestic servant, whose family had lived in the village for many years. Four years later in the autumn of 1890 Hannah married John Toomer from Codford, the next village three miles south. John and Hannah started their married life in Chitterne Road, Codford, where John was an agricultural labourer on one of the farms. In April 1891 Walter was five years old and Hannah had mislaid a couple of her years being 23 and the same age as John.

By March 1901 the family had moved to New Barn Farm, at Hockley, where John was the stockman and Walter was groom to the farm horses on Twyford Down. Walters's maternal grandmother Mary Coles had come from Chitterne to live with them and when Mary died she was buried in St Mary's Churchyard, on 5 January 1913.

Living close to Winchester and The Hampshire Regiment, in June 1903, like many 17 year olds, Walter exchanged the drudgery of the farm for a shilling a day all found and a life of excitement in the Regular Army by convincing the recruiting sergeant he was 18 under the name of John Toomer. Possibly Walter Feltham had lost his birth certificate.

The 1st Battalion had spent 20 years stationed in India and South Africa and returned from the Boer War in June 1904, to be stationed in Portsmouth. In February 1908 this battalion moved to Colchester.

Walter served with the Colours for three years and in June 1906, 6877, Private Walter Toomer of the 1st Battalion The Hampshire Regiment transferred to the Reserve. He then resumed his rural life and on 5 September 1910 Walter Feltham (24) married Evelyn Yarndley (26) in Ifield, Sussex.

They returned to Walters's home village of Codford, where in April 1911 he was working as a cowman on one of the farms and Evelyn in domestic service.

Walter must have obtained permission to change his name because the next time we hear of him, 6877 (same regimental number) L/Cpl Walter Feltham had been recalled to the Colours at Colchester where the battalion was mobilised on 5 August, promoted sergeant and with the 1st Battalion moved from Harrow to Southampton.

On 22 August the battalion sailed to Le Havre on the Cestrian, disembarking early the next day and after a day's rest took the train to Le Cateau, then on 25th marched towards Solesmes to support the retirement of the 5th Division.

In late October the battalion moved to Ploegsteert in the flat alluvial land of the river Lys, where the water table is never far below the surface, just north of Armentieres. Life in the Trenches was difficult, the main trench was flooded and baling out continued night and day using ladles on 6ft poles.

> *"You throw the water over the parapet and it then drains back though the earth to the sumps you are emptying. When off watch you lie down in the water for a couple of hours. The communication trenches are half full of water so you either dash over the top and risk getting shot or wade waist deep in the trench."*[1]

Apart from a spirited defence of the line on 7 November (56 casualties) and an attack to straighten the line on 19 December (42 casualties) the Hampshires seem to have had a unspoken agreement with the Saxons opposing them to fire as little as possible at each other. Then after 21st, coming up to Christmas, it was quiet, apart from the sea of mud, rain, frost, fogs, lice, vermin and sudden death by sniper. It had rained continuously, cold winter rain; since 20 November, neither side used their artillery much, the only casualties being caused by machine gun or sniper fire.

On Christmas Eve 1914 both sides sang Christmas Carols in their respective trenches accompanied by the odd unnecessary burst of machine gun fire. At midnight all firing ceased as if by mutual consent, then about 5.00am the Hampshires and the Saxons opposite began fraternising in no-man's-land unarmed chatting and exchanging souvenirs tins of jam, mufflers and tobacco for wine and cigars. By dawn the East Lancs and Rifle Brigades had joined in. The Saxons took the opportunity to bury some of their dead who had been lying in the mangel-worsel[2] field since the first attack in October, this pleased everyone as the foetid smell in the wind had made everyone very sick.[3]

Over the Christmas period, 20-31 December, only four soldiers were killed and seven wounded, although 179 were admitted to hospital probably with the usual conditions - frostbite (if you let the frostbite get bad enough you got a Blighty), diarrhoea, trench foot and exhaustion.

At the end of 1914, of the 1,000 odd men of the 1st Battalion who came out to France in August with such high hopes, only six officers and 366 other ranks were still present. 274 men had been killed and 405 wounded.

Walter's amazing luck finally ran out at Broodseinde on 4 October 1917 when he was killed probably during the initial attack by our own ragged barrage. This was the Hampshires worst day when two companies, totalling 530 men, half the battalion, were in the attack. 50% of those were casualties, 84 killed or missing and 187 wounded. The attack started east of Langemark to attack first Kangaroo Trench, 350 yds away and then on to the Traqique Farm 500 yards further on. His Battalion Commander's war diary relates the events of that day:

1. *Troops were formed up on assembly position by 2 am. About 5 am the enemy commenced shelling the line of Double cotts, increasing in intensity until zero hour.*
2. *At 6 am our troops commenced advancing behind our barrage. They met with very slight shelling and machine gun fire from the enemy, but our barrage is reported to have been very ragged and responsible for most of the casualties suffered in the actual advance. About 30 prisoners and one light machine gun were captured in Kangaroo Trench.*
3. *The line of Beek Villas was reached at 6:51 am without any serious opposition.*

...

10. *At 7.30 pm on 5 October the Rifle Brigade took over the whole Battalion front and my companies were withdrawn into Support in the neighbourhood of Louis Farm. The night on the whole being very quiet.*[4]

We next hear of his widow Evelyn when a Clasp for his most well deserved Mons Star medal, having been under fire with the BEF, was sent to her in a little brown cardboard box in April 1920, to her home at 6 Queen Ann's Terrace, Leatherhead. There was possibly a small pension of about 15/- per week or roughly £100 in 2013 money.

Ralph Scaiff

References:

1. Diary of an Old Contemptible : From Mons to Baghdad 1914-1919, Private Edward Roe, East Lancashire Regiment, pp61-75.
2. Mangel-worsel. Also mangel-wurzel, a variety of beet cultivated as food for livestock.
3. Christmas Truce, by Malcolm Brown & Shirley Seaton, Pan Grand Strategy Series, ISBN 978-0-330-39065-1, Pan Books Ltd, 1999. Page 67 and pages 47 onward.
4. 1st Battalion Hampshire Regiment War Diary, Ref: WO-95-1495-0-477, Sheet 20 et seq/46.

George Collins

Private George Collins Royal Irish Fusiliers (1897 – 23 November 1917)

1917. *"This is the third year of War. Will it be the last? At least one may wish that it may be."* wrote Reverend Morris in the New Year's edition of the Parish Magazine. The year continued to unfold with labour unrest in Britain; widespread anti-war sentiments in Italy and Austria; mutinies in the French army (May-June) and the German navy at Wilhelmshaven (2 August) and finally the Russian Revolution, which enabled the transfer of German divisions from their eastern to the western front. After the war Lloyd-George wrote of 1917

> *"The federated nations were now facing their fifth campaign. They were all exhausted and all disillusioned. The war fever had burnt itself out long ago in all the warring countries. Enthusiasms had cooled down." and "Haig talked about "the fatigue of his forces"; he alluded to them as his "weary and depleted units", pleaded that "having been engaged on the offensive since the spring" his army had been unable to devote either adequate men or time to the organisation of the British Front for the defensive."* [1]

November. Disappointment and disillusion had penetrated to so many levels. George Collins, a 20 year-old Twyford man had miraculously survived since 1914, but things were not well with his battalion, the 1st Royal Irish Fusiliers. Their War Diary records that on the fifth of this month

> *"the death sentence on No.12609 Pte. G.HANNA was promulgated at BAROSSA HALL METZ by Captain and Adjutant W.SCOTT, M.C. This was the first death sentence ordered to be carried out in this Battn. since its arrival in France. Pte Hanna was only about 5 hours with the Battn. He having joined with a draft but when warned for the trenches, disappeared. Firing Party, under Lieut. G.REEVE. M.C. proceeded to Divnl. Hd.Qrs."* [2]

The sentence was carried out at 0640 the following morning. As if that wasn't enough, that same day the diary records that the trial by General Court Martial of 2/Lieut. P.G.H. MANSFIELD commenced. This distressing news would have spread rapidly through the battalion, discouraging many and adding to the dread felt at the prospect of another winter in the trenches, and this was a unit that in a fortnight's time was to be committed to a major offensive.

Rewind to peacetime. George Collins was born in 1897, the 5th child of William and Caroline Collins. We believe he was born when the family was living in Doncaster, although in 1911 Mother or Father completing the census reported that he was born in Bolton, as was the case for older brother Alfred, perhaps just an oversight, other sources do confirm Doncaster.

Anyway, although William and Caroline were West Country born, their early married life was spent in the North-West and Midlands, their children being born in Stockport, Macclesfield, Burnley, Bolton, Doncaster (George), Hull and Peterborough. In 1901 the children in the family comprised William H., Caroline, Bessie, Alfred, George and baby Arthur (11 months). Sadly by 1911, when the family was living in Twyford at St Mary's Terrace, there was no record of Arthur, but three younger boys, twins Edward and Fred, and Jack, respectively five and three years old, had arrived. By now George was 14 and was working for the Post Office as a telegraph messenger boy. His elder siblings were also working, Carrie and Bessie as laundresses[3], Caroline as a dressmaker and Alfred as a drapery shop assistant. William was a photographer. [Their home was recorded as having six rooms, nonetheless with two people visiting them on Census night, current residents of St Mary's Terrace may care to reflect on how a household of eleven fitted into the property as they were configured not long after building.]

Twyford Cross-roads and Post Office, circa 1915

Although at work, George had time for other activities and he was a member of Miss Hull's Bible Class, which would have provided a lively social group and sporting activities. Of this class we know that 36 joined up and they would all have known the nine who died.

George responded early to the call to arms. The Parish Magazine of November 1914 reports him as having joined the 15th Hussars. They were based at Longmoor, the other side of Petersfield, and had mobilised to France from there in August. George joined with regimental number H/19119 and we would expect him to have gone to France as a draft to reinforce the regiment which had been involved in the retreat from Mons and subsequent fighting.

This brings us to the matter of George's age. Several records give 1897 as the year of his birth, (although the census of 1901 made him a year younger) in which case he would have been 17 in 1914. This makes him one of the approximately 250,000 boys who joined up under 18, the rule was that they could join up when 18 but not serve overseas until aged 19. One of the reasons that so many boys got away with joining was that not everybody in the years before the First World War received birth certificates and I have been unable to trace one for George. But there was known to have been widespread collusion in disregarding the rules, given the general belief that the war would be over by Christmas. That collusion clearly extended to our own community which would have been fully aware of George's age. It was not to be until 1916 that a campaign by the Liberal MP for Mansfield, Sir Arthur Markham, highlighted the plight of underage soldiers; in a statement to the House he had said: "There has been fraud, deceit and lying practiced (sic) by the War Office." and parents were given the right to claim their boys back. [4]

Once the war had settled down into a static contest of limited manoeuvre, as a cavalry regiment, the Hussars would have served in the trenches, but were essentially used as '2nd-line' troops engaged in activities behind the front line. Before each planned attack they would bring up their horses closer to the front line to exploit any breakthrough, only to take them back again afterwards. They were frequently forming working parties for digging trenches and preparing defensive works. In 1915 they had the unpleasant task of collecting and burying the dead from the battlefield. Before long it was their lot to be scavenged for replacements for the infantry. The 15th Hussars provided numerous NCOs who were given commissions in infantry regiments, and whole regiments were taken out of the line to provide replacements for other branches of the service (Carnock pp 131, 141 and 159).[5] We have been unable to determine the exact circumstances in which George came to leave the Hussars, doubtless with these pressures there was a local, or more general, occasion in which troops were transferred between regiments. George came to join the 1st Battalion of the Royal Irish Fusiliers (RIF), the "Faugh-a-Ballaghs" (Clear the Way), where his regimental number was 18931. Brigadier Burrowes, historian of the RIF, recounts how on one occasion, in January 1918, the battalion received a draft of 65 men, composed entirely of Army Service Corps bakers.[6]

But he was ever in the minds of people in Twyford, in February 1916 the Parish Magazine reported George received a pair of socks from home. Perhaps we can deduce from this that he was in the trenches and his transfer to the Fusiliers had taken place.

Anyway, in November 1917 the RIF were part of 107 Brigade in the 36th (Ulster) Division. The battalion had already fought at Le Cateau, the Marne, the Somme and Arras. Now plans were being made for the offensive that came to be known as the Battle of Cambrai. The division was responsible for the extreme left, the northerly sector of the attack.

The battle started on 20 November. It was planned as a surprise attack, in a relatively quiet area of the front. It employed the usual tactics, namely a bombardment by 1,037 guns, loads of smoke and a creeping barrage. The new element was the deployment of 437 tanks. This was initially very successful and advances of up to five miles were achieved on the first day, a success that was greeted in Britain by the ringing of church bells. However progress slowed down and no general breakthrough was achieved.

The RIF became involved in the battle on the fourth day and were supported by five tanks, they were ordered to take strong points Lock no 5 on the Canal du Nord and so-called 'Round Trench', some 8-10 km south-west of Cambrai. These should have been reached by the tanks beforehand, but it was left to hard infantry fighting to actually reach these objectives. The battalion's war diary for the 23rd records:

> *"23-11-17 Weather fine. At 12-10 pm the Battn. were ordered into Assemble Positions to take part in a second phase of the attack which started at 10-30 a.m. On coming out of trenches, the Battn. came under heavy Machine Gun fire. It was reported by a tank that a strong point on the road to the assembly position had not fallen. To reach assembly position it was necessary to take this. It was therefore attacked. The Battn. sustained the following casualties:- 8 Officers and 225 O.R's and got as far as the German wire of the main position with 3 Officers and 30 O.R's including 6 wounded. The assembly position was not taken. The line was then advanced to ROUND trench, the Strong Point and*

No. 5 Lock on the canal. Battn. were relieved by 10th Roy. Irish Rifles and 8/9th Roy. Irish Rifles in Round Trench and No. 5 Lock respectively, about 10-0 p.m. Lieut. Colonel S.U.L. Clements was slightly wounded but remained at duty." [2]

We know that George was killed on the 23rd and conclude that he was one of those 225 who fell trying to reach these objectives.

One post-battle analysis of Cambrai concluded that, despite the element of surprise and the use of so many tanks, the battle was as deadly, evenly balanced and relatively futile as so many other Western Front offensives, with both sides having very similar levels of casualties, c. 40,000 including injured and prisoners.

For George it took a little while for the news to filter back home. In the Parish magazine for February 1918 the Reverend Morris announced that George was reported missing and believed wounded. Sadly George's family and friends would have held out hope for him for many weeks after his actual death, the records now show that George had indeed died in that attack, on the 23 November 1917.

George is recorded on Panel 10 of the Cambrai Memorial, at Louveral, which commemorates more than 7,000 UK and South African servicemen who died in the battle and whose graves are not known. He was awarded the 1914-15 Star, the British War Medal and the Victory Medal. He was 20 when he was killed.

Christopher Pope

References

1. "War Memoirs of David Lloyd George, 1917-1918"; Little, Brown and Company; Boston, December 1936.
2. War Diary of the 1st Battalion Royal Irish Fusiliers, The National Archives - ref WO 95/2502/2.
3. There were probably four laundries in the village at the time, so a fair number of employment opportunities. Stanley Crooks and Doreen Pearce describe them in "Twyford Ringing The Changes", George Mann Publications, Nov 1999 - ISBN 0-95-244243-4 at page 43.
   The last laundry was still active in 1962. It was owned and run by David Pumfrett. Laundry House in Highfield was the reception for laundry taken in or for collection, there was also a delivery van. David Pumfrett was very active in the community; he was chairman of the Parish Council and an active County Councillor. There is a plaque to his memory on the bank behind the bus stop (on the side of the road going to Colden Common).
4. C N Trueman The History Learning Site, (http://www.historylearningsite.co.uk/world-war-one/the-western-front-in-world-war-one/boy-soldiers/).
5. The History of the 15th, The King's Hussars 1914-1922 by Lord Carnock, M.C. (late 15th Hussars) The Crypt House Press Ltd, Gloucester 1932, pp 122, 124, 131, 140, 159.
6. "1st Battn. The Faugh-a-Ballaghs in the Great War", Brigadier General A.R. Burrowes CMH, DSO, pub. by Gale & Polden Limited, Aldershot.

Wm James Barnes

Private William James Barnes Dorsetshire Regiment (11 June 1881 - 6 December 1917)

He could do no more, he could do no less.

I was born in the Old House in the small village of Froxfield in the Meon valley on 11 June 1881. My mother Augusta registered my arrival in Petersfield on 16 July 1881 and I was christened by the Reverend Hosegood in Froxfield parish church on 10 July 1881. Family and friends were there as well as my mother and father James. He was a labourer in and around the village.

My early life centred round school and the many festivals and services of the church. I used to enjoy watching the men and boys' races at the Church Horticultural Show and my mother and sister joined in the sewing competitions. The Reverend Hosegood seemed particularly good at growing vegetables and often won prizes for them at the village show.

Like lots of children I didn't like school much; many pupils were often absent especially at harvest time and in the fruit picking seasons. I remember one day all the parents were called in by the Vicar and Headmaster after the inspectors had visited and told their children must attend school regularly; school was a lot better after that. We moved to Twyford shortly after Queen Victoria died.

I had always liked horses and ended up working near Twyford as a domestic groom. I would normally have expected to live in but I lodged with Mr and Mrs Smeeth in their small cottage in North Town, as the area north of Twyford House was generally known. My pay in 1903 was similar to that of farm labourers, about 16 shillings a week. Living in the country the food was wholesome, not like the folks who lived in the cities.

In the spring of 1905 I had one of the happiest days of my life, I married my sweetheart Amelia Charlotte Gray. She was a cook for Mr and Mrs Trimmer.

It must have been a big change for her, moving from Winchester surrounded by her parents, brother and six sisters to our tiny cottage in North Town, Twyford. Her father, Horace, made and sold ginger beer.

We enjoyed living in our cottage and getting on with our humble jobs of groom and cook. Sadly we had no children.[1]

When war broke out in 1914 hundreds of thousands of younger men in their teens and twenties volunteered. I was 34 and continued to work with horses on the home front.

In 1917 after three years of near stalemate in the trenches in Northern France, the British Army was depleted by the enormous number of casualties, so I, like many older men, was conscripted. I enlisted at Winchester barracks, joining the First

Battalion Dorsetshires, my regimental number was 18283. After several weeks of training at various locations in southern England, we were ready for posting to France. During that training we learnt that our battalion had been the first to be attacked by the Germans with mustard gas on Hill 60 in the Second Battle of Ypres.

On arrival in Belgium we were stationed a few miles back from the trenches near Poperinghe. We saw many wounded soldiers being transferred back to field hospitals. There were also many soldiers who had been relieved from the front line to give them a chance to recover before being sent back to the trenches; they looked very tired, hungry and haunted.

We were moved to Brake camp near Passchendaele in late November where we stayed for a few days before being ordered into the trenches near Wurst Farm. The first couple of days of December were busy. On 2 December 1917 our commanding officer Cpt. Stayham gave the order for us to go over the top to try to regain land lost in previous weeks; after fighting all day through barbed wire, foul water filled shell holes, endless clinging mud and enemy fire we were ordered to retreat to our starting positions in the stinking filthy cold trenches. The 4th and 5th of December were quiet during the day, a few shells landing during the night; these shells killed one or two of our men and wounded several. December 6th was similar, quiet during the day, the shells coming in during the night ...

Private William James Barnes died of wounds on 6 December 1917 aged 37 years.

He is buried at DuHallows ADS (Advanced Dressing Station) Cemetery near Ypres, in Belgium. The Medal Roll records him as recipient of the War Medal and the Victory Medal.

David Snoswell

Reference:

1. There is no record of children being born to William Barnes in the Twyford Parish register or in the Census Record of 1911.

Notes:

1. Pte. Barnes widow, Amelia Charlotte received two payments from The War Office; Outstanding Pay of £7 2s 6d in May 1918 and a War Gratuity of £6 0s 0d in November 1919. Very approximately £705 and £600 respectively.
2. It has not been possible to find a record of Pte Barnes widow, under her married or maiden name, in the local parish records. It is possible she remarried in 1928 in Southampton.
3. Many of the regimental documents of the Dorsetshires were destroyed in the London Blitz in the Second World War.
4. The title of this piece is taken from the memorial order of service for my great uncles Pte. Arthur Cecil Snoswell and Pte. Ernest Edgar Snoswell, both of the Queen Victoria's Rifles who died in the First World War.

William Eades

Private William Eades Machine Gun Corps (1882 - 19 May 1918)

William Eades was a Twyford man, through and through. He followed his father, Henry (1835-1888), and one of his brothers, Harry (b. 1873), into service as a gardener at Twyford School as soon as he was old enough. Born in Twyford itself, as his father had been, William had three older brothers and two older sisters. William's mother, Dulcibella (1840-1919), was also local, having been born in Colden Common. He was baptised in St Mary's Church in the village on 11 June 1882.The family lived in North Twyford, in a cottage near St Mary's Church. When William's father died in 1888 they moved to the Old Parsonage. At the age of 25 William married Ethel, originally from Salisbury. The newlyweds moved into their own 4-roomed cottage near to William's mother. A year later they were blessed with a daughter, whom they named Ethel.

When the call came for volunteers, William joined the Hampshire Regiment, as many of his contemporaries would have done. He undertook initial infantry training, and then, when in October 1915, the War Office proposed the formation of a single specialist Machine Gun Company (MGCs) per infantry brigade (withdrawing gun teams from battalions), William was mobilised into the Machine Gun Corps, being assigned the number 62913. After basic infantry training, William would have travelled to the MGC depot and training centre at Belton Park in Grantham, Lincolnshire. From here his unit moved off to serve in France and Flanders. When the newly-formed companies arrived in France, they formed up at the Base Depot at Camiers. The Machine Gun Corps was evolving steadily over the few months from the end of October 1915. The eventual line-up would be: infantry Machine Gun Companies, cavalry Machine Gun Squadrons and Motor Machine Gun Batteries. William Eades was to be in the first of these – an infantry MGC.

Initially all units used the Lewis Machine Gun, which was an American-designed light machine gun. This could be fired from the shoulder and permitted new tactics to be developed. As the War went on more Lewis Machine Guns were supplied to each MGC. But there was also a need for heavier firepower. Use of the Lewis continued, but the Vickers Machine Gun became the established weapon for the infantry.

The Vickers .303 Machine Gun weighed approximately 42.5 lbs with 7.5 pints of cooling water to prevent overheating. The actual mounting weight was 48 lbs. Not only did they have to carry the gun and tripod, the poor soldiers also had to carry the belt boxes, which weighed 22 lbs with 250 rounds of ammunition in each belt.

The gun weight could vary according to the type of barrel casing and whether 'lightening' had been carried out. The overall length of the gun was 3 feet 8 inches and its cyclic rate of fire was between 450 and 600 rounds of ammunition per minute. Therefore, while one member of the eight-man gun team carried the gun, another would carry the tripod and the other six would have laden themselves down with belt boxes to be sure they would be able to carry out an effective performance once the gun was set up. The operation of the gun was recoil and fuzee spring. This latter tiny item, worked the crank handle up and down. There were 28 possible 'stoppages' on a Vickers, including a broken firing pin, fuzee, etc. but every member of the MGC had to be familiar with these and effect a rapid repair. The Number 2 operator carried a parts bag with a few tools and smaller items as spares. The broken part would be handed to Number 3 operator, who either replaced it or repaired it later. The barrel of a Machine Gun had to be replaced after 10,000 rounds because the rifling would be too worn to continue. It would take two to three minutes to replace a barrel. The Vickers fired 25 rounds in a normal five second burst. Members of the MGC believed the Vickers was the best weapon, provided it was kept oiled and the water jacket was kept full of water – even dropped in the mud and covered in muck it would continue to fire, unlike a number of other machine guns.

British Vickers machine gun crew wearing PH-type anti-gas helmets. Near Ovillers during the Battle of the Somme, July 1916. The gunner is wearing a padded waistcoat, enabling him to carry the machine gun barrel. Imperial War Museum photo Q3995. Note that the left hand soldier has an MGC badge on his shoulder.

With each new campaign, tactical use of Machine Guns was improved with infantry MGCs benefiting from artillery control techniques developed over the previous three years. When the infantry advanced the Machine Guns, which would have been placed initially up to 1,000 yds behind the front line, were then brought up swiftly as soon as enemy positions were captured.

William Eades' Infantry Machine Gun Corps was most likely engaged in the Battles of the Lys, Flanders. This was the third German offensive called Operation Georgette. Their purpose was to cut off British Second Army at Ypres by capturing key railway and supply routes. The British and French manpower was solid, with reserves arriving in time to hold the penetration. The action was in several parts:

- *Battle of Estaires, 9 – 11 April 1918*
- *Battle of Messines, 10 – 11 April 1918*
- *Battle of Hazebrouck, 12 – 15 April 1918*
- *Battle of Bailleul, 13 – 15 April 1918*
- *First Battle of Kemmel, 17 – 19 April 1918*
- *Battle of Bethune, 18 April 1918*
- *Second Battle of Kemmel, 25 – 26 April 1918*
- *Battle of the Scherpenberg, 29 April 1918*

Hostilities continued throughout May, and there was subsequent action at La Becque on 28 June 1918, and the capture of Meteren by British and French troops on 19 July 1918.

William Eades came through these actions until he was wounded, and had to be evacuated back to England.

Through the period from October 1915 to the end of the War, 170,500 officers and men served in the Machine Gun Corps, with 12,498 being killed. William Eades was one of the 49,500 soldiers in the MGC to be wounded.

When William was repatriated, he was transferred to the King George Hospital. This was an emergency wartime facility created in Stamford Street, Waterloo, in what is now the Franklin-Wilkins building of King's College, London. Over 70,000 military personnel were treated there between 1915 and 1919, including innovative plastic surgery cases. There were 1,850 beds available at any one time, all funded by subscription (£41,250 was raised by December 1914, with Queen Alexandra providing the first bed). There is little detail of how William Eades was injured, but he succumbed to meningitis on 19 May 1918. He was taken home to Twyford, so as to be buried in the churchyard that was only a few hundred yards from where he had lived and worked.

William Eades' gravestone can be seen in Twyford St Mary's churchyard. It is at plot no K.4, one of four Commonwealth War Graves headstones in the churchyard.

Steve Bailey

References

1. www.longlongtrail.co.uk
2. www.machineguncorps.co.uk
3. http://www.1914-1918.net/hospitals_uk.htm
4. www.iwm.org.uk

Thomas Wm Knight

Private Thomas William Knight Devonshire Regiment (18 October 1899 - 31 May 1918)

Early Life and Family

William Thomas Knight was born on 18 October 1899 in his parents' cottage in the High Street, Twyford. He was christened five weeks later, on 26 November 1899, in the parish church of St Mary the Virgin.

William's mother was born Rosa Sillence in Sherfield, Hampshire in 1859. In 1890 she married William Shadwell, a publican, in Alresford. He had been born in Cheriton in 1844 and in 1891 was working as the landlord of the "Brewery Arms" in Bank Street, Bishop's Waltham. The couple had three children – William born in 1891, Rosa in 1893 and, finally, Sarah in 1894. Sadly, Rosa's husband, William, died in 1897 at the age of 53, leaving her with three young children.

Two years later Rosa remarried. William Thomas Knight, who was born in Winchester in 1857, is listed as a general labourer on young William's birth certificate but two years later, on the 1901 census, his occupation is recorded as a butcher. On the same census, Rosa is listed as a 'laundress'. William took on Rosa's three other children, which might explain why he changed his occupation and, possibly, why his son, William Thomas Knight, soon became known as Thomas. William Knight died in March 1910 (coincidentally, also at the age of 53) and was buried on the 25th, Good Friday, in Twyford parish churchyard.

Come 1911 the family was still living on the High Street, Rosa was working as a 'charwoman', her eldest son William Shadwell (20) was a stable helper, her eldest daughter Rosa Shadwell (18) a laundress and her younger daughter Sarah Shadwell (17) was employed as a general domestic servant. Thomas Knight was 11 years old and a pupil at the village school in Twyford. He was a regular member of Miss Hull's Bible Class and, shortly before the outbreak of war in May 1914, he was confirmed in Compton Parish Church. At some point before 1917, Thomas was employed by Twyford Preparatory School as a member of the gardening staff.

Rosa Knight continued to live in Twyford after the war and died in April 1945 aged 86.

The War

In March 1917, at the age of 17, Thomas was called up and enlisted at Winchester as a private, number 74067, in the Devonshire Regiment. Earlier in the war, a soldier had to be at least 19 years of age to serve in a war zone. However, an extension of the Military Service Act on 10 April 1918 allowed soldiers aged 18 years and six months to be sent overseas as long as they had had six months training. After a year of training, Thomas left for the Western Front in the spring of 1918 to join the 2nd Battalion Devonshire Regiment in France.

The war on the Western Front was heading for a climatic end, unbeknown to the combatants at all levels. 1917 had closed with the horror of Passchendaele and its tremendous casualties on both sides. It had also seen the collapse of the Russian efforts following the Revolution and a cease-fire agreed with the Germans. This allowed the enemy to withdraw its troops from the east and deploy them on the Western Front.

The German "Spring Offensives" were designed to defeat the Allies before the Americans, who had recently entered the war, arrived in force. It was one last tremendous effort that lasted from 20 March until the middle of July 1918, comprising five offensives. The enemy took much ground over a wide front, including all they had lost in 1916 and 1917. Each offensive in turn faded as the supply lines grew longer and the fighting troops lost the support and reinforcements they needed to sustain the advance. The main crippling factor became the loss of manpower. Between March and July the German casualties reached over one million. This was the last straw for them.

The 2nd Devons

Thomas' battalion, the 2nd Devons, was a regular battalion that had been serving in Egypt at the outbreak of war. They returned to England in time to join the 23rd Brigade, 8th Division and embarked for France in November 1914. They were involved in the final stages of the First Battle of Ypres and in 1917 they again fought in this area from July through to November during the third battle (Passchendaele).

The drain on manpower brought on by the 1917 battles and the lack of reinforcements necessitated the reorganisation of the BEF in early 1918. Before that time a brigade had been made up of four battalions and 23rd Brigade comprised the 2nd Battalions of the Cameronians, the Middlesex and West Yorkshire regiments, as well as the Devons. In February 1918 the Cameronians were transferred to 59th Brigade. The three-battalion brigade was still expected to hold the same frontage of line, if not more, thus requiring longer periods in the front trenches for each battalion. This was one of the factors that led to the initial rapid advances by the enemy during the Spring Offensives. The divisional reserves had also been pared to the bone and it was not until the middle of the year that the reinforcements required for the allied offensives would arrive in France. Throughout the Spring Offensives by the enemy, allied troops would be outnumbered not only in infantry but in artillery, by three or four to one.

Between 21 March and 30 April 1918 the 8th Division had suffered nearly 9,000 casualties which was its complete fighting strength at best. By this reckoning the division had also lost many of its replacement troops. In fact the 2nd West Yorks and the 2nd Middlesex, the other two battalions in Thomas' brigade, had been practically wiped out twice over. It was in this shape that the division looked forward to a long needed rest to give it time to recover and absorb its reinforcements. Sir Douglas Haig, in his despatches, made these comments:

> *"The 8th Division had been involved south of the Somme in some of the heaviest fighting of the year, and had behaved with distinguished gallantry. All these divisions (the 19th, 21st, 25th and 50th as well as the 8th) had but lately been filled up with young drafts, and, despite their high spirit and gallant record, were in no condition to take part in major operations until they had had several weeks rest".*

One of these "young drafts" was Private Thomas Knight.

These divisions were all combined to form IX Corps, and they went south to the Rheims area, which was a reputed quiet sector in the French line. They were located north of the River Aisne near Bois des Buttes.

The move took place during the first week in May. By the 12th Thomas' brigade, the 23rd, took over the left of 8th Division's front on a line a mile wide and about two miles deep from the front to the reserve lines. The troops were spread thinly over the frontage but this was accepted in a quiet sector and with precious few reserves available anyway, even in the battle zones. The Devons held their brigade front line until the 20 May for what was, in the light of recent events a pleasant contrast. Little activity occurred until 18 May when the enemy tried to rush a forward post but they were beaten back. On the 20 May, before being relieved, the Devons raided a German trench in retaliation but found it deserted.

The battalion strength was now increasing to near normal. No fewer than 28 officers had joined since Villers Brettonneux and the rank and file was somewhat below 800.

The 26 May found the 2nd Devons back in the forward lines north of the Aisne. With the West Yorks holding the front line, the Middlesex were holding the second line and Devons were in reserve. Rumours were rife about an impending attack by the enemy and all the signs pointed to this. Most notable indications were the increased movements in the German rear lines and an increase in enemy scouting and harassment patrols.

The Battle of Bois des Buttes

The 2nd Devons were located in underground shelters and tunnels of the Bois des Buttes, a small hill to the rear of the brigade's lines. The Third German Offensive – the Third Battle of the Aisne – began on the 27 May. At 0100 the whole area was saturated with high explosive and gas shells. The Devons were in the best position in the brigade but, even so, many were gassed despite being underground and wearing gas masks. The West Yorks and the Middlesex suffered terribly. The enemy infantry had moved off at 0345, quickly mopping up the survivors amongst the West Yorks and rapidly overrunning the Middlesex.

At first light, approximately 0400, Lt Col Anderson-Morshead, the 2nd Devons' commanding officer, ordered the battalion to deploy to battle positions. The companies appeared from their shelters into the growing daylight and found that the Aisne Valley was shrouded in mist. Little could be seen on the open ground to the front. As the battalion made its way forward it found that many of the trenches had been reduced to shallow hollows during the course of the three hour bombardment. From this point onwards the battalion was to suffer a steady flow of casualties from the continuous heavy shell fire.

B Company on the left occupied a line of partly blown in trenches looking North West. Overlooking the ruins of La Ville-aux-Bois was D Company occupying similarly damaged trenches in the centre forward position. To their right was C Company, including Pte Thomas Knight, covering the flat marshy ground to the north east. A Company was with the Commanding Officer in the trenches surrounding the hill top. Once the Commanding Officer had sent out the Companies, all communication with them was lost. From the outset the forward company commanders, all lieutenants, were on their own to execute the 6th Army order that *'not an inch of sacred French soil was to be surrendered'*.

Almost immediately after the Devons deployed, B Company came under attack. Out of the mist came wave after wave of attacks, each beaten off with heavy casualties. B Company's successes in beating off a surprise attack from a powerful force were the first examples of the determined defence against great odds that was to characterise the battle.

The Fight for the Hill

Subsequent attacks on all three forward companies followed the same pattern except that as the mist burnt off with the rising sun great execution was carried out by the Lewis gun teams who were *'sweeping down great numbers of Germans'*. The longer ranges after the mist had disappeared meant that the Devons, in the centre of the breakthrough, were able to disrupt the move forward of enemy artillery and stores essential for their continued success. The positions in Bois des Buttes, now recognised by the Germans as a point of stubborn resistance, drew the attention of the German Imperial Air Force. Planes machine gunned and bombed the Devons at the edge of the wood and dropped smoke markers to direct the German field guns. Cpl Wotton, a survivor from C Company, recalled his section quickly learnt to change position after the over-flight of a German aircraft as it would invariably be the harbinger of another salvo of accurate shell fire.

Out-flanked on the left and severely reduced in numbers, C and D Companies were forced back into the wood. Young inexperienced troops, many in their first battle, having endured so much shelling, losing so many of their officers, NCOs and fellow soldiers, could have been forgiven for heading for the safety of the river line as quickly as possible. But the Devons made the Germans fight for every inch of the wood.

The remains of C Company, on the right, were forced to change position when it became apparent that 24th Infantry Brigade were no longer protecting their right flank and that a German battalion, probably from the 7th Reserve Division, was advancing on them from the east. The surviving officers and NCOs agreed, if necessary, to fight to the last man. C Company, at this stage only forty strong, was split into two. One group to give covering fire while the other was to charge the enemy, as this seemed to be the only way to break up the attack. The Germans were nearing the trenches when, on orders, the small party of Devons charged forward with a wild yell towards a whole enemy battalion. For better or worse the brave Devons never came to blood their bayonets, being stopped by an old barbed wire entanglement hidden in the bushes and long grass. They took up fire positions and continued to fire at the Germans who deluged them with grenades, machine gun and rifle fire.

A section in Martin Body's analysis of the regimental War Diary for this day reads:

> *"Pte Knight and five other men from C Company were one ... group who found themselves in a short stretch of old trench with Germans all around them. Quickly they formed a rough circle and 'blasted away'. When an opportunity presented itself they broke out and occupied another trench further back and continued to shoot down the advancing Germans. It is a great shame that there were so few survivors to bear witness to the heroism of small groups and determined individuals such as these men from C Company."*[1]

A mention of an individual private like this is very unusual in battalion diaries and, perhaps, indicates just how brave Thomas Knight was.

The 2 Devons were completely cut off from their line of retreat across the Aisne Canal. They continued to hold out and in so doing allowed the 25th Division time to come forward to reinforce the remnants of the 8th and 50th Divisions. By a supreme effort they formed a defensive line on the canal to allow an orderly retirement of neighbouring divisions. This respite was dearly bought by the 2 Devons, who lost 23 officers and 528 men, practically the whole of the battalion positioned north of the Aisne.

Although Thomas' date of death is given as 31 May 1918, it is highly probable that he died on the 27 May. Many of the huge number who died between the 27 and 31 May were given the latter date. Certainly, Thomas, like the many young men with him, did not fail his country and regiment in their time of need.

For their gallantry and endeavour the battalion was awarded the French Croix de Guerre, the first British unit to be so honoured, and one of only twelve during the Great War.

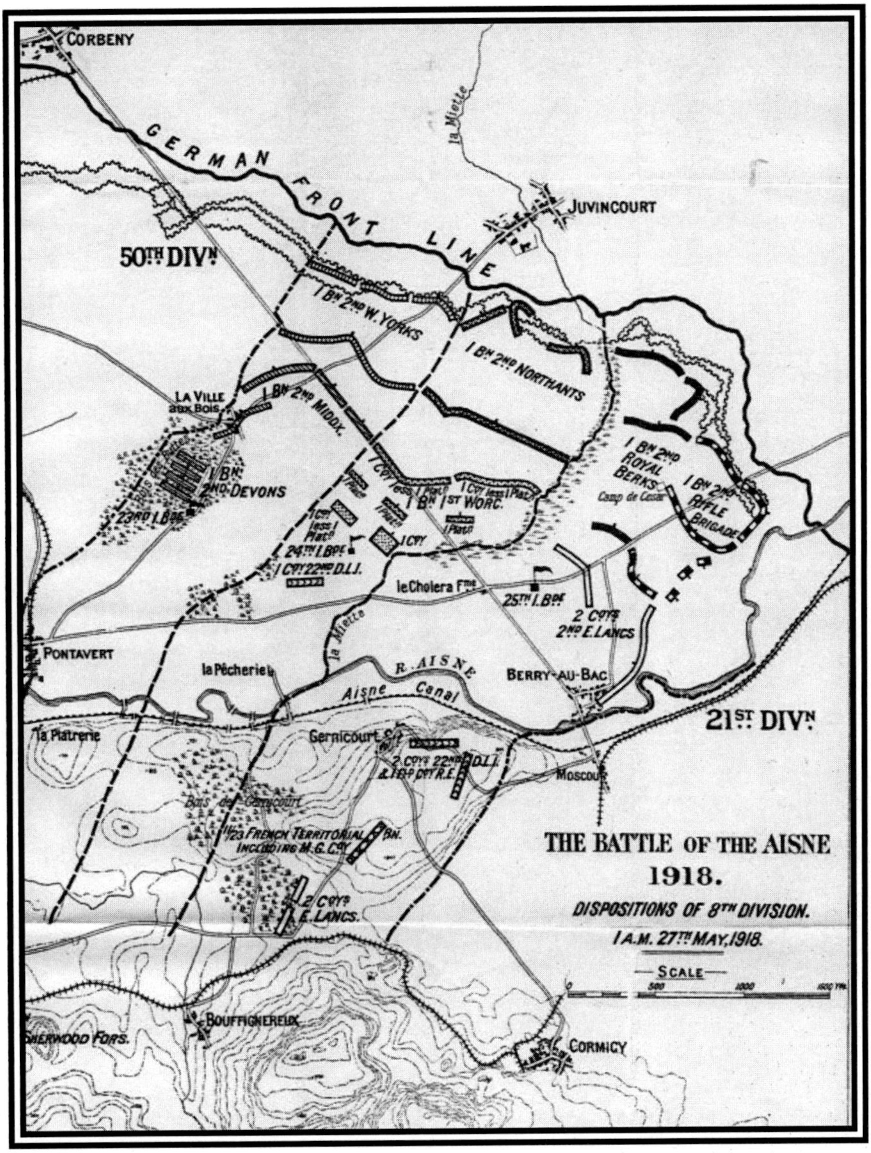

Some 80 of the Devons were able to escape from Bois des Buttes, but they hadn't finished fighting. The next few days saw a continuous fighting retreat, with groups of soldiers from all units combining to fight a more powerful enemy. To their everlasting credit they fought a far superior force to a standstill. Over the eight days following the opening attack on Bois des Buttes the Germans drove the Allies back from the Aisne to the Marne, finally coming to a halt on 4 June when their efforts petered.

At the end of the retirement the 2nd Devons had two officers and 90 men remaining. As the citation for the award of the Croix de Guerre had said of the 2 Devons:

> *"the Officers and men responded with one accord and offered their lives in ungrudging sacrifice to the sacred cause of the Allies".*

Like many more in the campaigns of the Great War, Thomas Knight has no known grave. He is commemorated by name on the Soissons Memorial that is located on the River Aisne where Thomas saw his last days. On this memorial there are 3,987 names of missing British soldiers, lost during the offensives in the Aisne area during 1918.

The Memorial Plaque or "Dead Man's Penny" issued to Rosa Knight after Thomas' death and still kept by a family member.

Andrew Keeling

References:

1. The 2nd Devons War Diary, Paperback - 21 Oct 2012 by Martin Body, Pollinger ISBN 978-1905665846

Herbert Tring Sapsed

Corporal Herbert Tring Sapsed RAF (18 September 1889 - 20 June 1918)

Herbert Tring Sapsed, known to his family and friends as Bert, was born in September 1889 in Wooburn, Buckinghamshire. He was eldest of eight children of William and Florence Sapsed and was christened at St Paul's Church, Wooburn on 20 October 1889 when he was two months' old. His middle name of Tring was his mother's maiden name.

His father, William, was Alfred Gilbey's coachman (of Gilbey's Gin fame) and before Bert was born his family lived in the servant's quarters at The Kennels at Berghers Hill - the residence favoured by Mrs Gilbey - and later The Stables, Wooburn House. The 1891, 1901 and 1911 Census's all show the family living in Berghers Hill, Wooburn.

Bert joined Wooburn Infants School in May 1893 and then went on to the Church School. The family worshipped at St Paul's Church and Bert became a sergeant in the Church Lads' Brigade. In the 1911 Census Bert is shown employed as a second footman in the household of Alfred Gilbey.

On 10 August 1914 Bert, aged 25, was appointed Police Constable 182 in the Buckinghamshire Constabulary in Slough. In 1914 military tension was rising in Europe. On 4 August Germany invaded Belgium as a means of accessing and invading France. Due to Germany's refusal to retreat from the invasion Britain had no option but to declare war on Germany and the Great War commenced.

On 8 September 1914, after initial training in the Buckinghamshire Constabulary Headquarters in Aylesbury, Bert was posted to the Southern Division and stationed at Slough.

Like many young men at the time, Bert volunteered for military service and on 27 July 1915 he was released by the Chief Constable of Buckinghamshire, under the provisions of The Police (Emergency Provisions) Act 1915, and joined the Royal Naval Air Service (RNAS, Rank No 207084). On joining up this 24 year-old was 5 feet 10½ inches tall with brown eyes, dark brown hair, a fresh complexion and a tattoo on his left arm.

His first posting, 15 September 1915 to 16 May 1916, was to HMS Canning[1]. She was a "Kite-Balloon Ship", to our ears somewhat of a paradox, but in reality the Canning was a mobile platform providing the balloon observation facilities that had become commonplace on the Western Front. She was assigned to support the landings at Gallipoli. She would manoeuvre into a suitable position, just off the Turkish coast, to enable targets and fall of shot on land to be observed, and then communicate instructions and results back to the guns further off-shore. As an Air Mechanic, and from 1 August 1917, a Leading Air Mechanic, Bert would have been responsible for repairing and maintaining the winching equipment and the balloon itself. The Canning received a battle honour for her service in 1915 in the Dardanelles campaign.

In December 1915 she was at Salonika involved in the intricacies of Greek politics and the question of the forts of Karaburnu. G Ward Price records that:

> *"The seizure of the forts was, indeed, an operation which needed careful preparation, for our naval captive balloon in H.M.S. "Canning" had been up every day taking photographs which clearly showed that the Greeks were busy building new gun-emplacements. We later found that they had also laid in a stock of armour-piercing shells of recent pattern."* [2]

The information provided by HMS Canning contributed to the forts to be taken by the allies without loss of life on 28 January 1916.

On 17 May 1916 Bert was transferred to HMS Ark Royal[3]. Coincidentally on 28 May, Canning was secured alongside Ark Royal exchanging hoisting gear and equipment, so Bert would have been able to renew old friendships. He was on Ark Royal for 19 months. She was a Seaplane Carrier, craning aircraft overboard to enable take off and recovering them afterwards. After some service nearer to the front line supporting the landings and earlier actions, she was deemed too vulnerable to U-boat attack to risk in open waters and in May 1915 was withdrawn to Imbros where she became in effect a depot ship for all aircraft based there. For much of the time Bert was on her she was based at Mudros acting as parent ship to No 2 Wing, RNAS.

Towards the end of 1917 Bert returned to the UK, at a time when the air services (RFC and RNAS) were being reorganised into the Royal Air Force (RAF). Bert was swept up in this reorganisation and he became a corporal in the Discipline Branch of the RAF.

HMS Ark Royal – Seaplane Carrier

By the time he returned from the War, his parents had moved to The Stables at Twyford Lodge, Twyford, near Winchester, still working for Alfred Gilbey. In the book *'Twyford - Ringing the Changes'*, Rod Sherren of Compton, who was born at Twyford Lodge, recalls that during or soon after the Great War, a member of the Gilbey family lived there and left behind for his successor a cellar well-stocked with fine wines"!

Will and Alf Sapsed – two of Bert's younger brothers

Meanwhile, Bert's brothers had also seen much service. His younger brother, William (Nos: 01060 & 31528), was a signaller serving in France with the Hampshires and Pte Alf Sapsed of the Dorset Regiment had been wounded four times. In April 1915 the British Forces Post (BFP) printed Alf's letter to his father telling how their ration party was sniped and he got a bullet in the arm: "I stopped a souvenir in the left hook as you used to call it ... I was carrying the Spratts' biscuits on the old left shoulder in a tin box which shone up in the moonlight ... They began pinging at the old tin ... I thought it was getting time to be missing and get down, when I felt the claret running down the old left hook". Alf survived the War passing away on 28 August 1987 and his headstone can be found in Twyford Churchyard.

On 19 January 1918, after Bert's return to England, he married his fiancée - Ethel Annie Kipping - in Marylebone, London. Sadly this marriage would only last for five months before his death. On 4 June that year Bert met with a seaplane accident. He died in Haslar Hospital on 20 June from a fractured skull, aged 28. It is not clear what happened but the BFP said *"we have it on the authority of witnesses of the sad affair that he nobly sacrificed his own life for his two comrades who were with him"*. Family folklore has it that Bert died as a result of an aircraft propeller 'kicking back' when he was trying to spin it to start the engine. The accident happened in England - perhaps at Worthy Down Airfield near Winchester.

He was buried with full military honours at All Saints Church, Leavesden, in Hertfordshire, where his Commonwealth War Graves headstone can be found. The gun carriage left from the home of his widow, Ethel. Bert Sapsed's name was not recorded on Wooburn War Memorial, probably because he and his family were no longer resident in the Parish when he died. He is remembered on the memorial tablet in St Paul's Church there, also on a plaque at the entrance of Court 2 of Aylesbury Crown Court - *"To the memory of those members of the Bucks Constabulary who gave their lives for their country in the Great War 1914-1919"* and finally on the wooden plaque at the back of St Mary's Parish Church, Twyford.

Researched by Vicki Dunlop and authorised by Gordon Patrick Sapsed (Nephew of Herbert Tring Sapsed)

Notes and References:

1. HMS Canning, Kite Balloon Ship, Mercantile Conversion, Y4.46 (fleet messenger pendant. no), N.16 (pendant. No.). Built 1896, 5,375 grt. Hired transport, red ensign 5.15-6.15, purchased 28.6.15, commissioned 29.6.15-27.6.16. In Mediterranean 1915-16, Scapa 1916-18, D/S 1917, attached to Flying Squadron in 11.18. Battle Honour Dardanelles 1915. Sold 21.1.20 to Greek owners. https://www.naval-history.net/OWShips-WW1-04-HMS_Ark_Royal.htm. (British Warships 1914-1919)
2. The Story of the Salonica Army, by G Ward Price, New York, Edward J. Clode, 1918. Chapter VII, para 6.
3. HMS Ark Royal, Aircraft Carrier, Mercantile Conversion Pendant Nos. N.80 (1914), N.07 (1.18). Launched 5.9.14 Blyth SB Co. 7,080 tons, 366(oa), 35(pp)x51x171ft. TE 3000ihp, 11kts. Armament: 4-12pdr, 4 seaplanes. Eastern Mediterranean 1915-18. Battle Honour Dardanelles 1915. Depot ship 1923, renamed PEGASUS 12.34, catapult ship 4.41, depot ship 1944. Sold 18.10.46 as Anita I. (British Warships 1914-1919)

Albert Chas Hickman

Corporal Albert Charles Hickman Army Service Corps (April 1892 - 27 June 1918)

Research in the Records is not very enlightening. The bare facts that emerge might be greatly enhanced from the memories and records of his family, who were very much a local family, if any can come forward after reading this note.

Albert was christened on 3 April 1892 in Compton, and was living in Queen Street Twyford with his parents at the 1901 Census, and was still there with them in 1911, when his occupation is given as carpenter journeyman.

Following the outbreak of War, he enlisted at Farnham. The military records are not helpful for his early service, but we know from the Parish Magazine lists that in October 1914 and November 1915 he was serving in the Leicestershire Regiment, latterly as a sergeant. This regiment had two battalions serving in France in the early stages of the war, both involved in fierce actions so it would have been at one of these where he suffered the wounds mentioned in his final Parish Magazine entry.

We do know that he was at home in September 1916 when, on the 9th, he was married, by Licence, at St Andrew's Parish Church in Farnham, to Florence Grace Durling.

Perhaps it was after his wedding he was posted to East Africa as mentioned, but it would not have been with the Leicestershire Regiment who had no representation there in the course of the war.

But by 1918 we have him back in the UK and Army Records show him as a corporal in the Army Service Corps, and his Unit (presumably at the time of his death) as the M.T. Depot at Norwood (Service Number M2/174811). The Parish Magazine in August 1918 summarises all we have been able to find of his army service and records his death at the Royal Herbert Hospital, Kidbrook, at the age of 26 years:

> *"He served in France and was wounded and then went to East Africa, where he served for over a year, and where his health gave way. Returning to England he seemed to be recovering, but an operation becoming necessary he was taken to the Royal Herbert Hospital Kidbrook, and passed away on June 27. He was laid to rest in our churchyard on Tuesday July 2."*

With the benefit of his Death Certificate it now seems likely that the operation mentioned by the Revd Morris was an appendectomy, a procedure that, at the turn of the 20th century, was by no means commonplace or straightforward. The cause of death recorded was "1. Appendicitis Peritonitis 8 days 2. Bronchopneumonia 8 days." and while this was perhaps the last straw to carry him off, it seems likely that his wounds from France followed by service in the tropics meant his health had become a major problem for him.

His wife Florence survived him for many years, and after her death in 1967 was buried with him in Twyford Churchyard, at plot no. K.4A. They share a gravestone that is recorded by the War Graves Commission as a war grave. They had no children.

The Medal Roll shows Albert as receiving the British War Medal and the Victory Medal. Florence would have received these after the war.

The dates on his tombstone in Twyford Churchyard are given as 1890 – 1918, presumably on the basis of information given by his widow. However, 1890 is inconsistent with the Census records, which are quite illuminating.

The 1891 Census shows Albert's father – also named Albert - living in Compton with his parents, single, aged 23, a carter; in the adjacent dwelling, Manor Farm, was living Mary J Green, also single, aged 26, a servant. As the Censuses for 1901 and 1911 record Albert's age as nine and 19 respectively, and he was christened on 3 April 1892, one would deduce that he was born after the date of the 1891 Census, 5 April 1891, and before 3 April 1892.

The Marriage Certificate gives Albert's age as 25. If this is correct, it would imply a birth between 6 April 1891 and 9 September 1891, and therefore a pregnancy at the time of the 1891 Census. If however Albert was born between 9 September 1891 and 3 April 1892, - and in view of his christening being on 3 April 1892 and it being customary to christen very soon after birth, birth in or about March 1892 would seem likely – Albert would have been only 24 years old at the time of his marriage.

Albert's parents compound the confusion, when completing the 1911 Census form. This required the inclusion of the number of completed years of the marriage, which number was initially shown as 19, but then amended to 20. With Albert appearing as a 19 year son, the amendment to 20 is explicable, but inconsistent with the 1891 Census which showed both parents as single. So far no record of any marriage has been found.

Exploring the family history further, the Hickmans were very much a local family. Albert's great grandfather Peter Hickman (senior) (1782 – 1852) was baptised in Hursley, married in 1806 in Hursley to Ann Hazelby, (1786 – 1858) a Hursley girl, and appears in the 1841 Census in Compton, and the 1851 Census in Twyford. They had at least five children, of whom Albert's grandfather Peter Hickman (junior) (1821 – 1900) was the second son.

Peter Hickman (junior) was born in Compton and appears in Compton in the 1841 Census, in St Cross in the 1851 Census, and then in Compton in every Census from 1861 to 1891, and was married to Sarah (maiden name unknown), who was also born in Compton. They had a daughter Elizabeth and at least three sons, Walter, Charles and Albert (senior). Walter married Angelina from Braishfield, and then lived in Compton next to his parents. In the 1891 Census, Peter Hickman (junior) is an agricultural labourer, and his wife Sarah and Walter's wife Angelina are laundresses, while the three sons Walter, Charles and Albert (senior) are all carters. By the 1901 Census Albert (senior) has become a brewers drayman, and is still a brewers drayman in 1911.

Albert's wife Florence's family came from Chatham, where her father James Durling worked in the dockyards as a hammersman or blacksmith. She was the eldest of five children, and in the 1911 Census she appears in Farnham, living as a boarder, with employment as a packer. Her presence in Farnham is presumably the reason why Albert enlisted there. She died in Basingstoke.

Michael Biddle.

Editor's Note

1. The Royal Herbert Hospital, named after the Secretary for War at the time of the Crimean War, was an army hospital built in 1865 on Shooters Hill a mile or so East of Greenwich. It was built in the pavilion style much approved by Florence Nightingale, with plenty of air and natural light. At its peak it had 15 wards accommodating 650 beds. Albert's last care would have been professional and up to date. The building remained a military hospital until 1977 following which it was redeveloped into a residential scheme now known as the Royal Herbert Pavilions.
2. The RASC MT unit at Norwood was the base for another of our men, Lance Corporal Alfred CARPENTER, buried in the churchyard.

Bruce Hutchinson Campbell

Lieutenant Bruce Hutchinson Campbell Gordon Highlanders (16 November 1878 - 18 September 1918)

Bruce Hutchinson Campbell came from a distinguished military and political family. His grandfather had conducted a Military Mission for Palmerston and had a successful military and political career in Canada. His father, Edmund Alexander Charles Campbell served in the British Army in India where his regiment, the 92nd, the Gordon Highlanders, had been one of those that suppressed the Indian Mutiny. Edmund's service followed this. He met Bruce's mother, Ellen (Nellie) Lind in Meerut, Bengal, India. They married on 10 March 1874. Bruce was born in Binfield, in Berkshire, on 16 November 1878. Within the family, Bruce was affectionately known as 'Hutty' (in keeping with his siblings: elder brother Edmund was known as 'Ebby' and younger sister Henriette was known as 'Etta').

We know that Bruce started as a pupil at Twyford School in 1889. In 1891, the Census shows that Bruce (aged 12) was living with his parents at Bridge House, Shawford, together with sister Etta, and brother Hugh, and three servants. Information from the Twyford School Archives tells us that Bruce was laid low by German Measles for the last three weeks of the Michaelmas Term of 1892, and he could not represent the School in the last two matches of the season. In the Summer Term of 1893 Bruce is photographed proudly in the Cricket 1st XI at Twyford School, just prior to moving on to Portsmouth Grammar School.

The 1901 Census gives the family as living on the Hazeley Road, with Bruce not resident on the day of the Census. Family members present were: his father and mother, brother Samuel (now aged 26) and sister Etta (aged 18). Sadly, Bruce's father was to pass away the following year, aged only 57. By the time we reach the 1911 Census, the family has moved to Rosedell in Twyford, where Ellen, Bruce's mother, is head of the household. Living with them are Bruce's older brother, Edward, and sister Etta. In addition, they now have Bruce's maternal uncle, Montagu Lind, living with them. Montagu Lind is described as an 'artist' in the Census, but he must have found it hard to make a living this way and he is listed in the Edinburgh Gazette a year later as a bankrupt! He is released from bankruptcy in 1913.

Early information on Bruce Campbell's military life is a patchwork: from his application for a temporary commission in 1915, it seems that he had already served three years in the Royal Berkshire Volunteers as a private, resigning when he moved away from the area. He had worked as a 'Brewer's Traveller' (1911 Census), and this is likely to have coincided with a period of time living in Berkshire. At the time of his application he was employed in the Army Pay Office in Winchester. The application form also tells us that he was unmarried, and that he was not able to ride! His employer in the Pay Office wrote: 'Mr Campbell has done very good work under me here. He possesses high intelligence and is a good business man'. Also on the application form for a temporary commission, against the question: 'The Branch of the Service in which desirous of serving', he entered Army Service Corps.

Anyway, despite his choice, in his mid-thirties, Bruce Campbell came to join the 11th Bn. Gordon Highlanders, his father's regiment, as a Temporary Second Lieutenant. In the course of training however, he was transferred to the 12th Bn. Argyll and Sutherland Highlanders, which was a Service Battalion formed to replace the professional and Territorial Forces. In September 1915 this battalion embarked on a long journey through France ending up on the Macedonian Front, also known as the Salonika Front, in November 1915.

This deployment was at the request of the Greek Prime Minister who had sought assistance of the British and

French in Salonika (now known as Thessalonika). The area had long been under the control of the Ottoman Turks. The objective was to help the Serbs in their fight against the Bulgarian Army (Bulgaria, neutral at the outset of the war, later aligned herself with the Central Powers). Two brigades (14,000 British and 34,000 French troops) were sent but arrived just too late to influence the early phase, when the Serbs were thrown back. The British were led by Sir Bryan Mahon and the French by General Maurice Sarrail. The decision was that the force should remain in order to help the security of shipping, as well as the supply lines to British forces involved in campaigns such as in Palestine. They became known as the British Salonika Force. This was by far the worst time to be establishing a base in the region: the strong and steady autumn rains would be followed by the extremely harsh winter. The major work of the first few months was arduous physical road building and other essential construction work, as well as creating effective defensive positions. A major fortification was built eight miles north of the city, consisting of a defensive line about 60 miles across and labelled the 'Birdcage' due to the overwhelming quantity of barbed wire deployed.

Unfortunately, there was little appreciation back in Britain for the campaign, calling it a 'sideshow'; this lull in action led to the press ridiculing the force, calling them 'The Gardeners of Salonika' because of the contrast with the many engagements in France and Belgium. In fact, the Bulgarians maintained a continuous bombardment of heavy shells from the hills, and there was a significant loss of life due to the conditions and the terrain. Malaria, dysentery, heatstroke and then influenza gave cause for serious concern to all commanders. There was significant loss of life. [Stanley Spencer was posted to this front, recording the experiences later in his murals at the Sandham Memorial Chapel near Newbury. Well worth a visit.] But the British Salonika Force continued training and was steadily reinforced. A major action was organised by General Sarrail, using two Russian brigades and a very strong Italian division, on 30 July and 10 August 1916 respectively. This began with heavy bombardment of Doiran, and the capture of Tortue by the French on 10 August and Horseshoe Hill by the British on 18 August. At the same time this enabled the British to cross the River Struma in several places and fortify, while the Italians took over a large portion of the Krusha Balkan sector. The enemy, however, used a surprise attack to the right bank of the Vardar against the Serbs to take the initiative back, forcing the French to transfer troops there immediately. As a result of changes in strength, the British effectively had to take sole responsibility for the front from Vardar to the mouth of the Struma.

Our Polyglot Army in the Balkans - L. To R., Back Row—Annamite[1], Frenchman, Senegalese, Englishman, Russian, Italian, Serbian (Part Hidden), In Front---Cretan, British Indian.

Early 1917 brought the vicious Balkan winter, preventing either side from any major adventure. Minor skirmishes and attempts to gain ground continued, but so did deaths from malaria and other diseases. There were 162,517 malarial cases among the British in Salonika. In an effort to reduce the loss of life in summer of 1917 the British withdrew from the foothills of the Struma region, as did their opposition the Bulgars. This created an enlarged No Man's Land of between 12 and 20 miles in width in the Struma valley.

In the main city itself, Salonika, another tragedy unfolded on 14 August 1917, when an old woman in the Ilan Mermer quarter, while frying her afternoon meal, accidentally set fire to her kitchen and then her house. The strong 'Vardar' wind soon fanned the flames, which caused the Great Fire that burned for a whole week! About 1/3 of the total population of 180,000 residents were rendered homeless by this catastrophe. The British troops could only help partially to put out the fire, as there was a totally inadequate water supply. But they were very active in constructing a refugee camp and servicing other essential means for those to survive after the disaster.

There was very little prospect of change at the end of 1917, unless factors from more distant theatres of war had a bearing. This was exactly what proved to be the case in 1918: many German troops were withdrawn from the Balkans with the Russian collapse, and the Bulgars did effectively lose heart.

Exactly how Bruce Campbell fitted in to this scenario is complicated by ill-health and injury. On his 'Casualty Form – Active Service'[2] key events outline his activities in 1916:

- 22/5/16 Campbell leaves Devonport for Port Said
- 31/5/16 He arrives in Egypt, proceeding to the School of Instruction at Zeitoun
- 12/8/16 Campbell moves to the Officers' Base Depot
- 24/8/16 He travels to Salonika from Alexandria
- 6/9/16 Campbell joins his battalion.

On 24 March 1917 Campbell was admitted as a casualty to the 79th Field Ambulance, and thence to the 31st Casualty Clearing Station on the same day. We do not know whether he was injured in battle, but he was then transferred the next day to 28th General Hospital in Salonika with bronchitis. Various entries in the Casualty Form show that Campbell was not generally well enough to return to active duty for over a month. He rejoins his battalion in the field on 15 May 1917. Shortly afterwards, on 1 July, he was promoted in the field to Temporary Lieutenant; this appeared in the London Gazette on 15 December.

Over the next six months Campbell served in the region with his battalion and for a period in 817th Divisional Employment Company, before moving to the Base Depot in Salonika on 21 July 1918 to begin 21 days leave back to UK, effective from 26 July.

Let us look at the final campaign. In the spring and early summer of 1918 there was an active redistribution of the allied troops. The new commander of the French (and overall commander of Allied Armies), General Adolphe Guillaumat, began to lay plans for a major offensive in September 1918 that would coincide with the proposed offensive in France. The 12th Corps, still occupying the Doiran-Vardar sector, was strengthened by more Greek troops. The responsibility now included both the British and the Greek stretches, pushing the range of defensive coverage from 90 miles to 135 miles. The offensive started with a heavy artillery bombardment from 1 September, attention was diverted from the Allies' main objective. A further bombardment then followed on 14 September, along the whole front from Monastir to Doiran. This permitted Franco-Serbian troops to take the enemy's first and second lines. British troops, together with French and Greeks, began an attack over the next days of the 'Pip' Ridge and also a surprise attack along the eastern shore of Lake Doiran.

On 12 September, just as the general bombardment switched to the specific heavy artillery attack on the front from Monastir to Doiran, Bruce Campbell arrived back in theatre following an extended period of home leave, beyond the allotted 21 days. In view of earlier information, we might expect that Campbell had continued to suffer from health problems, and needed to delay his return. He arrived back in Salonika on 14 September 1918, moving up to rejoin his battalion on the 16th.

The battalion was heavily involved in preparations for the offensive and the fact that Campbell had just returned from leave a day or two before this final push made no difference; he was straight into the action that was to prove fatal for him.

On the 18th the War Diary listed Campbell as one of the officers in A Company for the operation, which was due to start the following day. This was a tough assignment, as the aim was to draw the enemy into retaining sufficient reserves there so as to weaken their position for the Allies' main attack. Through this significant action at 'Pip' Ridge the Allies then could take Petti Couronne, Teton Hill and Doiran Town.

The events of the 19th started at 0315 with the assaulting companies approaching the wire in front of the enemy lines. They pressed home the attack at 0515. Initially a measure of penetration was achieved, when it was discovered that the front line trenches had been abandoned but a heavy artillery barrage then ensued, accompanied by traversing machine gun fire from a concealed concrete emplacement which *"severely depleted our ranks and caused the attack to waver* ..." (War Diary, Report on Operations Couronne Sector, page 1). A later note, at 0930 on 19th, estimated the number of enemy machine guns on the Tongue and Sugar Loaf at about 75[3]. Although the struggle continued there was a feeling that, due to the terrain and the conditions, neither attacking force could establish a more permanent foothold over the enemy's positions.

We know that it was during this engagement that Bruce Campbell was mortally wounded. He died on that day, 19 September 1918, before he could be evacuated to any of the medical facilities established in the rear. For the battalion the casualty list was just as horrendous as those others we have encountered on the Western Front. Of 17 officers and 500 men who went into the action, four officers and 148 men were reported Missing, and 12 officers and 125 men Wounded and 12 Sick (in action). Campbell was one of the four Missing officers; the paperwork later recording the stark details: 'Reported wounded and missing in the field' (reported on 24 September 1918) followed by, 'Now reported Killed in Action - body found' (reported on 10 October 1918). He was 39 years old.

The French and Serbs pressed home the advantage, taking the whole of the Vardar valley, cutting off the enemy's communication routes. The Bulgars retreated, pursued by the Greeks and British. Campbell's battalion went on to storm the Beles, the 4,000 foot high mountain range north of Lake Doiran. On 25 September an open roofed car was seen driving towards the Allied lines, with a white flag held aloft. The surrender of the Bulgarian armies at Doiran led to full cessation of hostilities in Salonika on 30 September.

Bruce Campbell was posthumously awarded the Victory Medal and the British War Medal. These were sent to his mother, Ellen. Ellen Campbell lived at Rosedell, in Twyford, to the ripe old age of 83, passing away in 1937.

In his Will, Bruce Campbell left everything to his sister, Etta, the record showing a sum of £656 12s 5d paid to Henrietta Blanche Gwendolyne Campbell on 12 April 1919.[4]

Bruce Hutchinson Campbell was buried at the Doiran Military Cemetery, in the north of Greece close to the Macedonian border and near the south-east shore of Lake Doiran. The Grave Registration Report shows his to be plot no. 30, the CWGC reference is: III.D.32. The Headstone Schedule, shows the standard text engraved on Bruce Campbell's headstone. Nellie subscribed to have additional words engraved: 'WELL DONE THOU GOOD AND FAITHFUL SERVANT', which also appear on the oak tablet commemorating her son placed on the south wall of St Mary's Church in Twyford.

Steve Bailey.

References:

1. The Story of the Salonica Army, by G Ward Price, New York, Edward J. Clode, 1918. Chapter XVI, para 15. Annam (Vietnamese: An Nam or Trung Kỳ, alternate spelling: Anam) was a French protectorate encompassing the central region of Vietnam. Before the protectorate's establishment, the name Annam was used in the West to refer to Vietnam as a whole. Vietnamese people were referred to as Annamites (Wikipedia).
2. War Office: Officers' Service File B H Campbell, WO 339/44023, comprising Form MT 393 Application for Appointment to a Temporary Commission P1040644-6, Casualty Form –Active Service P1040644-2 and other material.
3. War Diary, 12th Battalion Argyll and Sutherland Highlanders - WO 95/4886
4. National Probate Calendar (Index of Wills and Administrations) 1858-1966

Other Sources:

1. Dictionary of Canadian Biography Volume X (1871-1880)
2. National Probate Calendar (Index of Wills and Administrations) 1858-1966
3. Edinburgh Gazette, October 25, 1912
4. London Gazette, 25 July 1913, p. 5401
5. British Army Medals WO 372
6. Twyford Burials 1837-1950, p. 58
7. Census Returns 1891, 1901, 1911
8. Mann, Arthur James. The Salonika Front (A & C Black, 1920)
9. Hampshire Chronicle
10. Commonwealth War Graves Commission (CWGC)

Twyford Parish Hall, 1915

Henry P Parrott

Private Henry Peter Parrott Lincolnshire Regiment (20 November 1898 - 26 September 1918)

Henry Peter Parrott was born in the Parish of St. Mary's, Putney on 20 November 1898. In the 1901 Census the three year old was still living there with his father Thomas Joseph Parrott (1857-1926), mother Amy (nee Starling, 1872-1921), and older brother Percy Montague (1897-1991), who is also mentioned in Twyford records. There were two older siblings, Maud Kate aged 19 years who worked as a book keeper, and brother Thomas William a 14 year old school boy. These were probably children from Thomas Parrott's first marriage to Louisa S K Bown who died age 39 in 1896.

Thomas Parrott was a journeyman butcher, and the 1911 Census finds the family living at Ferndale[1] in Brambridge in the Parish of Twyford and Owslebury. In addition to Henry Peter, now recorded as Peter, aged 12, and Percy Montague the family now included Leonard G. (1901-1987) and Vera M. (born 1902). A fourth brother Jack Gurney had been born and died in 1901.

But the family were likely to be 'in transition'. An annotation on the Census Form mentioned that Thomas was 'Out of work', so perhaps it was job search that brought the family to Twyford shortly thereafter. It was soon enough for Henry Peter to settle into the Twyford community, where we know he was a member of Miss Hull's Bible Class and would have enjoyed all the social interaction of that group. At the time of his death, on 26 September 1918, just 46 days before the end of the War. The family's address was recorded as High Bank, School Road, Twyford

My interest in Henry Peter Parrott was aroused by the question: how did a Twyford man born in Middlesex come to serve in the Lincolnshire Regiment, my home County? The 1st Battalion Lincolnshire Regiment was stationed in Portsmouth when War was declared on 4 August 1914 being part of the 9th Brigade of the 3rd Division of the First Army. It comprised 1,007 soldiers of whom 30 were officers, and mobilised for war on 14 August 1914 landing in Le Havre, France. Did Henry Peter Parrott enlist immediately, and mobilise with this battalion, rather than join the Hampshire Regiment whose 1st Battalion was stationed in Colchester on 4 August and reached Le Havre on 23 August 1914? Tantalisingly in addition to his Service Number with the Lincolnshire Regiment (51417) he also had a number (2629) with the Hampshire Regiment which I have been unable to trace further.

Does his War Record help to answer these questions? The Armed Forces Records indicate that he died of wounds on 26 September 1918, while serving with the 1st Battalion Lincolnshire Regiment in France and Flanders. He is buried in the St. Sever Cemetery Extension, Rouen, where his gravestone is marked "In Memory of Private H.P.Parrott, 51417, 1st Bn Lincolnshire Regiment who died on 26 September 1918 age 18." This should be "age 19 years", and adds to the mystery about when he enlisted. If he had enlisted in August 1914 he would have been three months short of 16. Like many he would have falsified his age if he had enlisted directly with the Lincolnshires in Portsmouth at the outbreak of war.

By 1918 the Lincolnshire Regiment had seven battalions in France with the 1st Battalion still active. The Regiment lost 8,800 men in the First World War, and across Britain men from wherever were enlisted into whatever regiment, perhaps to help disguise the fact that each County and location was losing so many men, and it is more likely that Henry Peter Parrott had actually enlisted in 1916 when he would have been 17 or 18. In late Summer 1918 the "100 days Offensive" of a series of key battles began which was finally to break the Hindenburg, or Seigfried, Line and lead to the end of hostilities on 11 November 1918. The 1st Battalion Lincolnshire Regiment was involved in a number of these battles including the Battle of Epehy on 18 September north of the St Quentin canal. The War Diary for the 1st Battalion Lincolnshire Regiment shows that between 18 and 20 September 1918 they were in position near Sorel-le-Grand and advanced on and took Vaucelette Farm which was their objective. The diary indicates that seven men were killed, 50 wounded, 20 missing, and 16 sick. Private Parrott was presumably one of the wounded. He was evacuated towards Rouen 200 km away but died, to be buried there in St. Sever Cemetery extension alongside 8,646 other dead. The vicar announced Henry Peter's death in the November 1918 edition of the Parish Magazine, which doubtless landed on peoples' doormats practically in the week the Armistice was declared.

Henry Peter Parrott's story is one of so many of the "Tommies", be they Twyford men, or from wherever, who made the ultimate sacrifice, but the strength of whose courage and unselfishness of whose gallantry, although never promoted nor decorated, cannot be measured by records and our interpretation of them.

Andrew Brooks.

Editor's Note

1. We believe Ferndale to be the house next door to the car park entrance to the Dog and Crook, eight doors along Brambridge from Highbridge Road.

Ernest Reason

Staff Sergeant Ernest Matthew Reason Army Service Corps (16 April 1882 - 14 January 1919)

Ernest Matthew Reason was born on 16 April 1882 in Grays Thurrock, Essex. He was the youngest of six children born to Henry Reason and Mary Ann Burke. His father, a mariner, died around the time of his birth aged only 43. Ernest and two of his three brothers joined the Navy and were based in Portsea, Portsmouth. His brother William was given a place at the Royal Hospital School in Greenwich, a naval training school for orphan sons of mariners.

Ernest spent his younger years in Grays Thurrock. Aged eight he was living with his mother and older sister, who worked as domestics to support the family, and ten year old brother Harry. By the time he was 18 the family had moved to live in Portsmouth.

In 1900 Ernest joined the Navy. When he joined up he stood 5 feet 5½ inches, with brown hair and hazel eyes and had been working as a cellar man. He was rated as a Domestic, probably today a Naval Steward. His Navy Number was 358535 and he was posted for shore work and to Portsmouth-based ships. In 1901 he was serving on HMS Spiteful, a 'B' class torpedo boat destroyer, a '30 knotter'. Launched in 1899, she was serving with the instructional flotilla when Ernest was with her. Later, in mid-1913, she was operating with the Portsmouth Defence Flotilla. However in 1903 Ernest left the Navy. The final entry in his record simply says "Shore no longer reqd." For his time in the Navy Ernest's 'Character' report was VG every year.

We're not sure what Ernest did next. Anyway perhaps he was most comfortable with service life, because by 1911 he was in the Army, as a baker with the ASC (Army Service Corps), based in Alverstoke at New Barracks, Gosport.

When the war came, Ernest went to France in 1914, as a corporal with the 3rd Field Bakery ASC. Field bakeries comprised an officer and 92 other ranks. One was mobilised for each division but they worked in the rear areas, behind the trenches, baking the bread for about 20,000 men each.

In 1917 Ernest married Elizabeth Ethel Smith, in Portsmouth. Elizabeth was born in 1887, a carpenter's daughter from Winchester. She grew up in 1 Park View in Shawford with her brother Albert and sister Bertha (future wife of George Mansell). She had been working as a domestic nurse for Captain Charles Burnett Woodham and his young family who were from the Portsmouth area (tragically he also lost his life in the war, in 1915). Ernest and Elizabeth went to live with Elizabeth's grandmother at Romanville in Twyford.

In the early part of the century, Italy had sided with Germany and Austria-Hungary, but when war broke out in August 1914 declared its neutrality. Eventually siding with the Allies, Italy declared war on Austria-Hungary on 23 May 1915. A series of very costly battles ensued and, following the German intervention to assist Austria-Hungary, Lloyd George became very concerned that the Italian armies would collapse and Britain, with France, sent reinforcements to the Italian front.

Ernest, who had survived on the Western Front, was now a staff sergeant with the 25th Field Bakery. This was part of XIV Corps which was reassigned to Italy and arrived there in November 1917.

The following year a big push on this front culminated in the decisive Battle of Vittorio Veneto (October - November 1918), which brought Austria-Hungary to the negotiating table and an armistice was signed to take effect on this front on 4 November.

After the Armistice, Ernest's unit remained in theatre when, only two months later, he suffered a tragic accident working in the bakery. A letter written to his brother William describes this awful event of 14 January 1919. The letter appears as closely as possible below, a few words of the handwritten original proved not possible to transcribe.

> *Dear Mr Reason,*
>
> *I am in receipt of yours dated 23.1.19. Re. your brother's death. It was very sad and every one of the company joins me in expressing our sympathy with you in losing your dear brother who as you say made your home his home until his marriage. On the evening of 14.1.19 about 11pm he was foreman in charge of the night shift and as usual about that time went to the pump house to start a motor for the water for dough making. A few minutes after it started a corporal who was attending to the ferments heard it stop again, as that was nothing unusual, the corporal finished his ferments about 5 minutes later and then went across to see if Staff Sergeant Reason required any assistance. On entering he found your brother lying alongside the motor with his waterproof coat and jacket wound tight round the shaft and pulled close round his neck and quite dead. 2 or 3 minutes later the Sergeant Major was on the spot when he was cut away and artificial respiration applied for some time. An ambulance car then*

conveyed the body to hospital where he was at once attended by the doctors who came to the conclusion that he was stunned by the fall when pulled off his feet and then strangled by his clothing before he could recover. He had not been carried round the fly wheel or shaft as the motor is very small and not able for that, just his clothing twisted tightly up. He had not had any pain as the knock on the floor had stunned him as could be seen by the mark on side of his head. It is supposed that after starting he had turned round to take something off the shelf alongside when the end of the shaft where the starting handle is put on had caught the end of his water proof coat and pulled him down striking his head on the cement floor and then twisting up his clothing until the weight of his body stopped it working in which position he was found. He was buried from the hospital with full military honours on the afternoon of 17 January 1919 in the cemetery of Montecchio Maggiore about 6 or 7 miles from VICENZA on the railway between VICENZA and VERONA. By the end of this month we are to have a strong iron railing round the grave with a wooden cross made by one of his friends on which will be placed a brass plate with inscription, after which I will send you a photo of the spot. I may state he was one of the best and most reliable of N.C.O.s respected by officers and men alike.

I am yours truly

J. Morrison Capt. T.D R.A.S.C

The photograph mentioned by Captain Morrison was forwarded as promised and we now have a copy of this. Some years later the crosses in Montecchio Maggiore Communal Cemetery were replaced by War Graves Commission headstones, Ernest's with the inscription "Until the day breaks". He lies with Private J Styles of the Gloucestershire Regiment, two Great War casualties in the civilian cemetery Captain Morrison mentioned. Ernest received Pip, Squeak and Wilfred, the affectionate names given to the three First World War campaign medals - the 1914 Star, British War Medal and Victory Medal respectively. Ernest was 36 years old when he died.

Ernest Reason's original grave, with the cross and railing mentioned in Captain Morrison's letter.

Elizabeth Ethel Reason continued to live in Twyford, at Rosslare in The Crescent. She died on 2 October 1943 and is buried in Twyford St Mary's Churchyard, where the inscription on her own gravestone includes reference to Ernest – "ALSO OF HER HUSBAND SERGT E REASON ACCIDENTLY KILLED IN ITALY 1919".

Vanessa Croucher

References

1. EMR Naval Service Record, The National Archives - Kew, ADM 188/544/358535.

Percy F J Allen

Driver Percy Frederick John Allen Royal Horse Artillery (7 January 1901 – 10 April 1919)

Percy Allen was born in Winchester on 7 January 1901 and was just three months old at the time of the 1901 Census when the family were living in St Maurice ward at 65 Middle Brook Street, Winchester, next to the Robin Hood Public House. This Public House may not have been the best neighbour for Percy's upbringing, as it subsequently lost its licence and was eventually demolished as part of "slum clearance" in the 1950's. Percy's parents were both aged 23 when he was born and John, his father, was a laundry carman and his mother, Eleanor (Ellen) was a washer laundress worker on her "own account". Percy was baptised on 7 April 1901 at the parish church of St John the Baptist, the oldest parish church in Winchester, in the area where John had been brought up. John was clearly a local man, with his father's occupation being a "soda water bottler" and several generations going back to East Stratton in the 1700's, whereas Eleanor had been born in Battersea and trained to go into Service at St. Jude's Home, Chelsea.

At the age of four, Percy attended St John's National/Church of England school in Winchester (opposite St John's Church) and by the age of ten the family had moved the short distance to 62 Water Lane, Winchester. At this time Percy also had a younger brother, Ernest William and two younger sisters, Edna (May) and Edith (Gladys).

When Percy was a teenager the family moved to Queen Street, Twyford and Percy was involved with village life and was part of St Mary's Bible Class under the supervision of Miss Hull. One record in March 1917 refers to Private B Hooton, of the London Scottish, stationed at Hazeley Camp, instructing and training the Class in physical drill and gymnastics in the Vicarage Tithe Barn, which culminated in a splendid display for family and friends. In June, Percy's brother, Ernest, was part of the gym display team in the Vicarage garden and maybe Percy's absence from this event was explained by his being too busy playing in St Mary's Bible Class Football Club, where he was one of the top scorers in the 1916/17 season!

From Miss Hull's album, illustrating the gym display in the Vicarage garden, June 1917

Percy had work as a labourer at a Gas Works when the First World War ended and shortly after his eighteenth birthday he applied to the Royal Horse Artillery (RHA) at Woolwich to join up as a driver. He would naturally have grown up working with horses due to his father's occupation, as well as his father joining the Royal Field Artillery as a driver, so this undoubtedly inspired him to join the RHA where, as a driver, he would have managed the horses drawing the guns and ammunition wagons. Indeed after the War many ex-servicemen became carmen, following their service as drivers. Percy was duly enrolled on or about 11 March 1919, his regimental number was 282864, and undertook training, where it is thought that he suffered from trench foot in his first few weeks and was admitted to Brook War Hospital, Shooters Hill, Kidbrooke, close to the Woolwich RHA barracks. Sadly there he caught influenza, (maybe not surprising, as the flu pandemic of 1918-19 killed 50 million people worldwide) and contracted pneumonia, which led to his death on 10 April 1919.

Brook Fever Hospital was requisitioned by the War Office and was operational as Brook War Hospital from September 1915 to November 1919, eventually becoming a general hospital, before finally closing in 1995. Like many sites around the country, the 29 acres became "Brook Village" containing luxury apartments and although few original buildings remain, the 20,000 gallon water tower that Percy would have noticed, is now an exclusive dwelling with spectacular views over London!

Percy was laid to rest at St. Mary's Church, Twyford on 17 April 1919, he is at plot K.13, marked today with a CWGC headstone, one of four in the churchyard. The Rev Harold Morris, Vicar of the Parish, took the funeral service, expressing deepest sympathy to Percy's parents, particularly as John, Percy's father, was still on his way back from India with the Royal Field Artillery.

After the war the Allen family continued to have highs and lows, one particular joyous event being the double wedding of both of Percy's sisters on Boxing Day 1934 at St Mary's Church, Twyford. Edith Gladys married John Coaker and Edna May married Thomas Wilfred Mansell. Sadly Edna May died barely two months later from Purpura Haemorrhagica, an illness similar to meningitis normally only found in horses, and is buried close to Percy in the Churchyard.

John (Percy's father) had his own laundry business in 1934, thought to have been at Crantock in Queen Street and both he and Eleanor outlived three of their four children. When John died in 1960, whilst still living in Queen Street, his ashes were interred in Percy's grave. Percy's mother, Eleanor, died the following year, having been at Wimble Hill Hospital, Crondall for some years. In 2015 Percy's nephew, John Allen (Ernest's son) was also interred in Percy's grave, so three generations are buried/interred together, the two John Allen's being grandfather and grandson respectively.

David Owen

4. THE MEN IN THE CHURCHYARD

Walter George Dale

Private Walter George Dale London Regiment (11 December 1873 - 4 July 1916)

Walter Dale was born on 11 February 1873 in Camberwell, South-East London. His parents were Henry and Fanny Dale, who already had three boys, Henry, Ernest and Arthur, who was three when Walter arrived. Walter was baptised the following February, on the 18th, at St George's Church there. Seven years later, in 1881, we see the family living at Arundel Drive, St James Road in Battersea and there has been a new arrival, another boy, six month-old Algar. Walter was at school at the time and this looks like a comfortable and settled family home. Henry and Fanny were both 40 and Henry was working as a "Distillery Traveller" and they were able to afford a servant, Clara Knight, who was living with them.

By 1891 Walter had struck out on his own. He seems to have settled on the hospitality trade and was working as a waiter in an hotel at 32 Dover Street, in Mayfair. He was living in and his manager at the time imagined he was 19 but in fact he was probably only 18.

In 1900, when he was 26, Walter married Sarah Tytherleigh. Her home was in West Ham and she was 23. They were wed in West Ham in the late summer. The following year they were living three or four miles away in Leucha Road, Walthamstow. Walter was working at this time as a Hall Porter again at an hotel, whether still in Mayfair we do not know. They were to start their family straightaway, their daughter Gladys Winifred was born the following year.

In 1909 we know that Walter and Sarah were living at 33 St Mark's Road in Camberwell and they are there in 1911 when Gladys was nine, Walter junior eight and Henry three. They also have a lodger, Victor Smith, he was a single man, 39 and working as a 'Printer in Charge'. Walter described his profession at the time as 'Club Steward'. Later that year the family moved to 18 Faunce Street in Kennington, a pretty tree-lined cul-de-sac with houses on three levels. Perhaps the attraction was Keyworth Primary School at the bottom of the road, with its separate gates with stone-carved inscriptions for 'Boys' and 'Girls & Infants'. Today houses in this street change hands for over a million pounds.

When war was declared Walter was 40 and with a wife and three children couldn't have been expected to join up straightaway. However the pressure would have built and in October 1915 he enlisted, (his regimental number (4479) supports this[1], and he would have been a volunteer. He joined The London Regiment, The Prince of Wales' Own Civil Service Rifles and was assigned to the 3/15th Battalion, the Reserve Battalion that was based in 1916 on Hazeley Down. Their role was to train new recruits and provide replacements to the active battalions, the 1/15th on the Western Front and 2/15th which went to Ireland in the spring of 1916 and later in June to France. New recruits went through a basic training programme for 3-4 months which could be followed by further specialist training as required. So for the early part of 1916 we can conclude that Walter was committed to training programmes with his regiment and would at least have been able to enjoy the spring and early summer sunshine on Hazeley Down.

However we can only imagine the strains and pressures up at the camp as 1916 developed. By late spring the Battle of Verdun had been grinding for months and the British were being called upon to engage the Germans elsewhere along the line. The Somme offensive was the response, due to start in July, and the Reserve Battalions would have been working at full pelt to get replacements to their front line regiments on the Western Front.

Walter was a casualty of all of this. At the time he was working as a chef in the Officers Mess, but doubtless this would have been in addition to other duties and training. The raw fact of his death is summarised on his Death Certificate, which stated that on Tuesday 4 July he "Killed himself while of unsound mind by cutting his throat with a razor." The Coroner's inquest was conducted on Thursday 6 July.

The report of the inquest describes how Sarah Dale gave evidence confirming that she had heard from Walter a week ago when he had seemed quite happy and three weeks ago he had been at home when he seemed perfectly happy, with no complaints. Sgt Harry Gayer of the battalion, who had been friendly with Walter since February, testified stating that Walter was "very sensitive". He recounted how on the Monday he asked Walter if he was alright, his initial reply was yes, but that later Walter had blurted out "I'm done, Sergeant". Gayer pressed Walter as to the problem and more came out: "The staff have worried me a little ... petty questions. There was an undercurrent of feeling which he could not explain. ... the previous Sunday evening songs were sung about him ... If I did not feel unwell tonight I should settle the matter as I know who is the leader." Gayer left it there at the time but after lunch on the Tuesday Walter, somewhat unusually, retired to his room, so that Gayer felt the need to visit and check on him, but Walter said that he was alright.

Later that afternoon Lance Corporal Chapman, passing by in the corridor outside Walter's room, heard unusual sounds, and, on going in, discovered Walter lying on his bed bleeding from wounds to his throat. No-one else had been in the room since Sgt Gayer had left. Private Wartnaby testified that he and Walter had been great friends and "he had never heard of Dale being ragged." He had been in the canteen on Sunday and Monday evenings and nothing was sung or recited that referred to Walter. The jury returned a verdict of suicide while temporarily insane.[2]

What a tragedy. We have a picture of Walter suffering in silence and shielding Sarah from the anxieties of his life in Hazeley. And then when it started to come out to Sgt Gayer, it was too late and the difficulties appeared insurmountable. At this distance it is impossible to assess the extent to which his suffering wasreal or imagined, although it is reassuring to learn that due processes were followed and with some sensitivity.

He was buried the following day, Friday. He was 42.

In the Parish Magazine for August our vicar, Harold Morris, wrote:

> *"And a further sad event during the last month was the death at the camp of Private W.G. Dale, 15th London Regiment, under extremely distressing circumstances. He was laid to rest with full military honours in our churchyard, Friday July 7."*

Doubtless Sarah was able to stay on for the funeral, but there is no mention of others there, nor any sign of the multitude that were to attend Douglas Small's funeral nine weeks later. Walter lies in plot J.19 in the lower churchyard, north-east of the clipped yew planted in 1902 for the coronation of Edward VII. The marker installed at the time has since been replaced by a Commonwealth War Graves headstone, one of four in the Churchyard. I have not been able to find Walter's name on any war memorials in South Lambeth. St Mark's Church is 12 mins walk from Faunce Street and Walter's name is not on their memorial, nor on any of the other churches slightly further away[3]. He is mentioned on the 'WW1 War Memorial for London', an on-line memorial for London's fallen soldiers of the First World War, and I am able to report that his name appears in the regimental history[4], which contains a list of all who served during the war, Walter's name in heavy type "representing those who died on Active Service".

In winding up Walter's affairs the army Register of Soldiers Effects resolved Walter's account out at £1/17/11 (doubtless outstanding pay and allowances) and this was remitted to Sarah in October that year. However the wheels of bureaucracy continued to grind small and slow ... and some three years later Sarah received the War Gratuity in respect of Walter, in September 1919, a sum total of £3/0/0.

Sarah lived a long life, dying in 1964 aged 87, in Bridge near to Canterbury in Kent.

Christopher Pope.

References

1. Army Service Numbers 1881-1918 http://armyservicenumbers.blogspot.co.uk/p/index.html.
2. Reported in the Hampshire Chronicle, 15 July 1916.
3. South Lambeth War Memorials, https://sites.google.com/site/southlambethwarmemorials/st-marks-war-memorial-kennington-oval
4. The History of The Prince of Wales' Own Civil Service Rifles. Pub/Printed by Wyman & Sons Ltd., Fetter Lane, E.C. for P.W.O. Civil Service Rifles, Somerset House, Strand, 1921, Appendix IX, p. 433.

Editor's Note

At the time suicide was a criminal offence and generally regarded as a sin, and shameful. This may explain Walter's speedy burial and why he was not included on memorials in his home area, even if they were told. It was not until 1961 that the law decriminalising the act in England and Wales was passed, so that those who failed in the attempt to kill themselves would no longer be prosecuted. During the war years reported suicide rates declined sharply and significantly. "Suicide rates in males steadily increased by 67% from 1861 to reach a peak of 30.3 per 100 000 by 1905. Rates then decreased to 21 per 100 000 in 1917 (during the First World War), increasing to reach a second peak of 30.3 per 100 000 in 1934, coinciding with the Great Depression." Suicide in England and Wales 1861–2007: a time-trends analysis, Kyla Thomas & David Gunnell, Int Jrnl Epidemiology (2010) 39 (6): 1464-1475. DOI: https://doi.org/10.1093/ije/dyq094, Published: 2 June 2010.

I have not been able to find any information about suicide rates in the armed forces during the war.

More recently suicide rates have continued to fall and for men currently are: "In 2015, the suicide rate in the UK rose slightly to 10.9 deaths per 100,000 population, up from 10.8 in 2014." Statistical bulletin: Suicides in the UK: 2015 registrations; ONS, Contact: Jodie Withers Release date: 2 December 2016

John Douglas Small

Private John Douglas Small London Regiment (March 1898 – 19 September 1916)

I first stumbled across it by chance..! It was tucked away in the corner of the churchyard surrounding Twyford's beautiful Parish Church and, being off the main pathway, it had long given up the struggle against ivy and long grass. I think it was the shape that caught my eye as I wandered absent-mindedly through that tall grass and I stopped, picked away at some of undergrowth that had attached itself to the headstone and, underneath years of neglect, there appeared some metal lettering affixed to the concrete face...

It read:

'In ever loving memory of Private John Douglas Small of the London Regiment 'Kensingtons'. Son of Albert and Emmie Small of Elfords, Hastings who passed away at Hazeley Down Camp, on September 29th 1916 aged 18 Years'.

The words said everything, yet told me nothing. Who was this young soldier who had been stationed at the big First World War pre-embarkation camp in the village? That, in the third year of that terrible conflict, this soldier, not long out of basic training, had died at such a young age was obvious... *but how and why?*

Had he made it to the Western Front and returned to die of his wounds? Had he been taken ill awaiting the move to the trenches of Flanders?... or was there a more sinister story behind this innocent headstone? More intriguingly, why did this soldier's grave have a private headstone whilst other soldiers who'd died at the camp, and were also buried here in Twyford's churchyard, have the instantly recognizable, white, official, military headstone with Regimental badge? *So many questions, but where to begin to find the answers?*

Having lain undetected for so long, the answers were not to be eventually found locally, however a letter to a local newspaper in the Hastings area appealing for information brought a breakthrough for me. Several Hastings residents remembered the family of John Douglas Small, then came the big tip-off: 'Douglas', as he was apparently affectionately known, had a younger sister who was actually still alive and living in a nursing home in Battle and, armed with this information, I made my way to Sussex to meet Constance 'Connie' Small. A former teacher and now in her nineties, this lovely old lady was as bright as a button and, obviously touched that I had taken over tending her late brother's grave, she talked to me about his tragically short life.

Douglas was her favourite older brother and on leaving school at 16, he took a job in his father's motor-vehicle garage. Called up at 18, he enlisted in Chichester as 6120 Private Small in the 13th (Kensington) Battalion London Regiment a Territorial unit known colloquially as the *'Saturday Night Soldiers'*. Following basic training, his Regiment was despatched to Hazeley Down, Twyford, in preparation for its transfer across the Channel to France and the Western Front.

But on the morning of the 26 September 1916, as the lads were called to muster at 7am ready for the 'off', Douglas could not be roused from his bed; the camp doctor was called and he was transferred to the military hospital at Haslar in Gosport down on the South Coast, where meningitis was diagnosed. Tragically he died three days later and his body was returned to Twyford and the Hazeley Down camp.

By his untimely death, Douglas Small was spared the horrors of the Western Front, but I asked Connie how her brother came to be buried in Twyford: *"My father made that decision. In those days getting around the country was not easy and as Douglas loved Twyford and was a popular figure around the village, my family thought it would be fitting for him to be buried there and a private headstone was bought".*

The 'War Casualties' listing in the Hastings & St Leonards Observer on 7 November 1916 confirmed her brother's popularity:

> *"Private John D Small was buried with full military honours in the Twyford Village churchyard. There was a very large attendance at the graveside: about a thousand military and civilians being present, including the Officers, NCO's and men of the Regiment and the Regimental Band".*

Meanwhile back to Hazeley Camp, where today an imposing cross, erected as a memorial to the tens of thousands of young men who passed this way, can be seen, set back from the Hazeley Road amidst the few remaining wooden barracks from the First World War that still dot the hillside.

As for the grave of her brother that Connie never got to see (our churchyard plot no K.19), it is now lovingly cared for in Twyford's little Parish church, by myself and latterly the War Graves Commission, its sad history now finally known!

Connie died shortly after I visited with my photos of her beloved brother's grave and I take comfort knowing I was able to show her where 'Douglas' was laid to rest and assure her his grave was now looked after and that each November a British Legion Red Poppy is placed upon it…

Brian Matthews

Editor's Note

In 1889 the County of London was created from 28 metropolitan boroughs and incorporated much of Middlesex, Surrey and Kent. This newly formed county had no Regular Army Regiment – multiple Volunteer Rifle Corps had formed in each of the counties surrounding the city which were now incorporated into the County of London.

In 1908 these battalions were merged as part of the Territorial and Reserve Forces Act of 1907 which converted the Volunteer force into the Territorial Force, and the battalions became the London Regiment. The Regiment is unique as each battalion has retained a measure of its original identity with distinctive badges and uniforms independent of the regular army. It was also the largest Regiment with 26 Battalions; the first eight designated as City of London and the remaining 18 as County of London Battalions. The 13th Battalion came from Kensington with a more full, formal title of '13th (Princess Louise's Kensington) (County of London) Battalion, The London Regiment' (https://www.forces-war-records.co.uk/units/4899/london-regiment/)

Alfred Carpenter

Lance Corporal Alfred Carpenter Army Service Corps (21 August 1887 – 20 February 1921)

Alfred Carpenter was born on 21 August 1887. The circumstances surrounding his birth were dramatic for the family. His mother was Rose Ellen Carpenter, daughter of John and Alice Carpenter, who in 1881 were living in the village in Twyford. She was ten then, with an older sister Annie and a younger brother William and sister Alice. But only six years later she was in the Workhouse in Alresford, the mother of a baby with no declared father. Alfred's birth was recorded almost a month later, Father's Name blank, indicative of illegitimacy and of how tough things were for the young Rose Ellen, aged only sixteen. We know nothing of the circumstances surrounding her leaving home, although at the time significant social stigma attached to illegitimacy [1]. Was it father, mother or both who were so shocked by the expected arrival of an illegitimate grandchild, or was it the general reaction of the village as a whole that made her leave home. We shall probably never know. However family relationships must have calmed down a bit over the next several weeks because by 23 October 1887 Alfred had been brought to Twyford to be baptised, in St Mary's Church.

So, Alfred was born in the workhouse in New Alresford. It still stands, to the south of the town on Tichborne Down. Parts of the buildings that remain have been converted into residential accommodation (now Headley Close, SO24 9XE). Understandably in later life Alfred, and his relations, chose to forget these beginnings, and all the formal documentation I have seen give his birthplace as Twyford.

Two years later Alfred's grandfather John died, the parish record showing him having been buried on 19 January 1889. Was it this that enabled the family to move on? Either way, just over a year later, when he was three, Alfred really was in Twyford, living with his grandmother Alice and her children Annie, William, Alice and Flora, essentially his maternal aunts and uncle, Flora only six years his senior. Alice's home was no 16 in the High Street. He was to stay in this household for his childhood and young adult life, Alice must have been a strong woman to keep this family together by herself. Things had improved for Rose too by the time of the next census, 1891, when, aged 21, she is living in Hyde in Winchester, working as a cook for the Kaines family.

Ten years later Alice's household was still together in the High Street, although her two eldest children had moved on. Alfred was 13 and at school. Doubtless for the reasons we have seen, he is reported as Alice's 'son'.

In 1911 Alfred was still living there, with grand-mother Alice and Flora, now 29. He was 23 and working as a domestic gardener. Their house had four rooms so things must have been a bit more relaxed at no 16 compared with earlier years when the family had comprised six.

When the war came Alfred didn't join up straightaway. Perhaps his mind was elsewhere, for in October 1915 he got married, to Lottie Rodaway, at Holy Trinity Church, Colden Common. Lottie (born in March 1886) was a year older than Alfred, an Otterbourne girl, daughter of William Henry and Mary Ann who had both been born in Otterbourne themselves. William Henry had worked in the brick industry for many years and in 1911 was the manager of a brickyard. Lottie was one of seven children.

On 9 December 1915 Alfred signed up. He is one of a few of our men for whom service records exist, the great majority of these having been destroyed in the Blitz, the so-called 'burnt records'. Anyway his attestation papers show that, at 28 years and five months old, he was 5 feet 6½ inches tall and a chest measurement of 36 inches with a two inch range of expansion. He was assigned to the Army Service Corps (ASC), to the Motor Transport unit and based at Grove Park, in North-East Kent. In fact he is posted to the Army Reserve, which I understand to mean that he was actually released home pending later re-call. His enlistment papers give Lottie as next of kin with an address of New Road, Colden Common.

Perhaps he was assigned to the Reserve as a holding measure while his deployment was worked out. The record is somewhat unclear as to whether Alfred was mobilised the following March, in 1916, or six months later in October. Anyway on the 31 October he joined the Grove Park unit and it looks as though his first task was to learn to drive a motor vehicle. On 8 January 1917 he passed the 'Learners Test' and on 16 February he was promoted to lance corporal, so he was doing well.

The Corps Alfred had joined played a massive part in Britain's war effort. The ASC became an enormous logistical organisation, it was their job to provide the food, fuel and the plethora of items of equipment needed by a modern, industrialised army (weapons and ammunition were handled by the RAOC, the Ordnance Corps). The vast majority of the supplies were sourced from Britain, requiring a terrific transport commitment. Using horse-drawn and motorised vehicles, railways and waterways, the ASC performed prodigious feats of logistics and were one of the great strengths of organisation by which the war was won. The Corps comprised Horsed Transport, Mechanical Transport, Remounts, Supplies (including bakeries and butcheries) and Labour Companies (which were really at battalion strength) and at its peak, the ASC numbered an incredible 10,547 officers and 315,334 men. Alfred's unit was the "No 1 Reserve MT Depot – Grove Park", the building was formerly a workhouse itself and included a large railway marshalling yard, taken over by the ASC for the duration of the war. Today there is still a fairly large area of sidings and carriage sheds adjacent to the railway station of the same name, probably even more extensive in 1914. It was also an ASC centre for driving training in Kent.

Following his promotion, the details of Alfred's military record are not very clear, and make me wonder whether in fact he was developing some health problems, because for much of 1917 he was in charge of the gardens at the Norwood Centre, something he was well qualified to do, but which may not have contributed that much to the war effort, and a year later, just before the armistice, on 10 October 1918, his record shows him as "Compulsorily transferred to xth (not legible) Branch Medically unfit for MT duties Dis not caused or aggravated by M.S." On 21 March 1919 his record includes the following - "No longer physically fit for War Service. XVI", XVI being the clause under Para 329 of Kings Regulations under which he was discharged. Alfred's condition was a perforated nasal septum, deemed as 'Non attributable', presumably to war service. He was judged to be 20% disabled and granted 6/10th of a Weekly Allowance for 41 weeks (inclusive of an allowance for one child).

Again the record is not very clear, the period from 19 October 1916 to 21 March 1919 is entered as "Home", suggesting that Alfred would have been at home for the birth of his and Lottie's son, Alfred Dinsdale, on 2 January 1919.

Sadly Alfred was not long to survive the birth of his son. On 20 February 1921 he died at home aged 33. His death certificate, recording that he died of a haemorrhage, was signed by Dr Marsden Roberts, whose picture hangs in the corridor to the consulting rooms in our surgery in Hazeley Road.

Alfred was buried three days later, on the 23rd, in plot L.15 in the lower churchyard, under the clipped yew planted in 1902 for the coronation of Edward VII. He is accorded a Commonwealth War Graves headstone, one of four in the Churchyard. Doubtless it was Lottie who selected the family inscription that appears at its foot, "Safe in the arms of Jesus".

The final question in my mind about Alfred's end was why, dying at home in 1921, was he regarded as a casualty of the war. There is the beginnings of a clue in the CWGC record[2] for St Mary's Churchyard; two other military graves are mentioned on the same sheet as Alfred's, W Shadwell and AT Conduct, buried in 1924 and 1925 respectively. Their entries are crossed out on this sheet in red ink and annotated 'Post War Burial "Not a War Grave"', implying that Alfred's was a 'War Burial' and a 'War Grave'. Critical however are the criteria adopted by the War Graves Commission for war casualty status, the most significant being date of death. For the First World War the Qualifying Dates were 4 August 1914 to 31 August 1921. Furthermore "The location of their death and the cause of death are immaterial to their qualification. They could have been killed in action, died of wounds, died of illness or by accident, died due to suicide or homicide or suffered judicial execution. CWGC treats all casualties equally and all must be commemorated under the terms of their Royal Charter."[3] So Alfred's death in February meant that the CWGC was able to accord him one of its memorials and include him in its register of the Fallen. Meanwhile however, and somewhat on a separate timeline, village preparations were in train to commemorate the Twyford men killed in the war. In July 1919 the Church Architect produced his design for the commemorative panels that we now know. In January 1920 the paperwork requesting approval was submitted to the Church authorities and shortly thereafter the memorial was installed. So, since these arrangements were done and dusted by the time of Alfred's death the following year, his name does not appear on our memorial.

Further correspondence in Arthur's file shows that Lottie continued to receive a pension by virtue of his military service. When Alfred died in 1921 Lottie's pension was 15 shillings. Lottie lived a long life and died locally in 1967, aged 80.

Christopher Pope.

References

1. "Such was the shame that families went to great lengths to keep their guilty secret under wraps ... Before the 20th century it was illegal for illegitimate children to inherit ...". Guardian On-Line, Saturday 14 April 2007.

2. Commonwealth War Graves Commission: 'Graves Registration Report Form' for St Mary's Churchyard.
3. The "In From The Cold Project" (IFCP) website,
http://www.infromthecold.org/war_grave_criteria.asp.
4. and also ex Ancestry
Census Records, 1881 – 1911
Army Attestation, Enlistment and Service Records.

The Alresford Union Workhouse in 1907

5. LIFE IN THE VILLAGE

Belgian Refugees in Twyford, 1914

As part of this project a review was undertaken of the Parish Magazines for the years 1914 to 1919. This revealed the wide range of charitable activities in the village to do with the war and the war effort which were new to me, and which I found interesting. I thought that readers might like to hear of some of the ways in which the village helped, apart from the men who were in the services already or who volunteered to serve.

The first little item which must have reflected a general anxiety, was a report in the September 1914 magazine that the Church Lads' Brigade had formed patrols to assist the police by giving information of unauthorised persons visiting outlying farms and houses in the district. There was, at the outset of the war in particular, a fear of spies although it seems that German espionage in Britain was neither widespread nor successful. There is no further comment about this activity, and I think the government acted very quickly to round up potential agents.

In the November 1914 issue of the Magazine there is the first mention of one of the important and ongoing commitments the village made. A meeting had been held on 20 October 1914 'to consider if anything could be done in Twyford to assist the Belgian refugees.' The background to this was the German advance on France through Belgium, which was part of the Schlieffen Plan and the immediate reason for Britain's declaration of war on Germany. Britain had guaranteed, with France, to maintain Belgium's neutrality. The German government saw no reason to accept their neutrality, and were determined to pursue their plans to attack France through Belgium and by outflanking the French armies achieve an early overwhelming victory. The Germans were considerably put out by the Belgian intransigence and resistance, and their advance through Belgium was accompanied by much brutality against the civilian population, producing a flood of refugees which numbered tens of thousands. There was a lot of public sympathy for the plight of the Belgians. To quote Michael Gilbert, Thomas Hardy wrote of his pastoral dream that the Belgian refugees would arrive in Britain with their bells and music:

Then I awoke; and lo, before me stood
The visioned ones, but pale and full of fear;
From Bruges they came, and Antwerp, and Ostend

No carillons in their train. Foes of mad mood
Had shattered these to shards amid the gear
Of ravaged roof, and smouldering gable-end.

At this meeting in October a decision was made to take an empty house on the Morestead Road and offer it until 25 March 1915 to the Mayor of Winchester. A committee was formed, consisting of; Mrs Gilbey, Mrs Roberts (the doctor's wife), Mrs Ratclife, Mrs Morris (the vicar's wife), the Rev Morris, and Mr Arthur Smith. The question of furnishing was settled by some generous offers to be responsible for a bedroom as well as many offers of loans of other articles. Donations of £17-9-0 as well as further sums to cover the rates and taxes were given. Mrs Roberts was the treasurer.

In December 1914 it was noted that there were now eight Belgian refugees dwelling in Twyford and the writer (presumably the vicar) says, 'one hopes that it is a real place of refuge to them after the hard times through which they have passed.'

A weekly collection of donations organised by Mr Gilbert, the schoolteacher, was in place, and by 18 November the committee had received £51-7-7, (expenses totalled £16-18-5). Some of the regular sums which were raised went to the National Belgian Refugee Fund organised by the Daily Telegraph. By January a further sum of £39-11-7 had been received. In the same issue of the magazine there was a letter of thanks from the refugees:

Ladies and Gentlemen, I take the respectful liberty of thanking you for all that you have done for us all in Twyford. We shall never forget the days that we have spent in your charming neighbourhood and which makes us forget a little the miseries we suffer. Vive l'Angleterre!! Vive La Belgique!!
Victor Eggers.

On 12 February 1915, there was a meeting of subscribers to the fund when the accounts showed £142-5-2 received, and £76-6-7 expended. It was resolved to continue the fund-raising and to take the house for a further three months. 'One can only hope that by that time the way may have been opened for these unfortunate people to return to their own country. It is hard to imagine what desolation they will have to go back to.'

In April 1915, as well as the regular statement of the accounts, it was recorded that Mr Eggers had found employment with a Mr Hodder of Winchester. His earnings went to the committee who retained part for 'future needs.' By May the income of the fund had risen due to wages received weekly, and as well as Mr Eggers, a Mr Van Herteryck was working for Arthur Smith at the Brewery Buildings. By June it was apparent that the refugees were practically supporting themselves, and at a meeting on 16 June the accounts showed a total of £198-15-11 received, with expenses of £105-18-7. With this healthy balance and the income from wages it was decided not to ask for further subscriptions for the present but to review the situation in September. 'The committee desires to thank all those who have come to the help of these unfortunate people.' The Rev Morris felt that a public expression of thanks was due to Mrs Ratcliffe, 'who had had the whole of the management of the refugees' house and had equally considered their comfort and the purses of the subscribers. She had done very kind and good work, and done it well.'

A statement of the accounts showed that as well as the larger subscriptions from the more wealthy residents in Twyford, Mr Gilbert's weekly house to house collection over the previous 33 months had raised £69-10-9 from 168 contributors, which had been divided between the Twyford fund, The Daily Telegraph Fund, and also for the relief of suffering in Belgium as well. (I am not sure how that was achieved). In September 1915, the PCC was asked for help towards the support of Belgians starving in Belgium, and the Fund sent a small donation from their reserve fund.

In November 1915 it was recorded that Jack Van Herteryck had joined the Belgian Army and was going to France for training. In December it was commented that 'our Belgian friends are going.' As well as Jack Van Herteryck, Mr and Mrs Eggers with little Jenny and her grandfather had moved to Farnborough (they had arrived on 31 October 1914). Mr Eggers had taken work at the Farnborough Aeroplane Works, and found a small house nearby with help from the Twyford fund to furnish it. The writer says that all were sorry to part with the Eggers and little Jenny who had been a general favourite. Mr Van Herteryck and two daughters were to remain at the house until Lady Day.

This appears to be the last note about the Belgians and the Fund and one must presume that the Fund was wound up and the remaining family became self-supporting.

Bruce Lees

Twyford Parish in the First World War

Before Christmas the Parish Magazine carried my first article in which I wrote about the efforts made in Twyford to care for Belgian refugees during the First World War using the Parish Magazine reports for the war years 1914-1918. But this was not by any means the only charitable work which the Parish made to help the war effort.

In the September 1914 issue it was reported that 'a small committee of ladies had met at the vicarage to arrange for some help to be given by Twyford to our soldiers and sailors by making useful clothing.' It was proposed that a fund should be raised, and garments ready cut should be given to workers at the Parish Hall on Tuesday and Friday mornings between 11 and 12 am. An immediate response had produced three dozen good shirts! The fund had produced £26 12s 7d of which £22 12s 7d was spent on materials. There followed a list of 33 subscribers.

In the November issue there is a list of garments made and sent off, for example 24 pairs of socks to the 'Yorkshire Regiment', and they had had a letter of thanks from Mr Geoffrey Gilbey (whose family lived in Twyford). Eighty-three names are now included in the list of subscribers and helpers including some names of families which are still, or until recently were, living in the area: Mrs Lampard, Mrs Jannaway, Florence Jannaway, Mrs Best and Maggie Dumper. Miss Hull's name is also there.

A month later it was recorded that the funds were exhausted so no more work was to be given out, over £39 had been spent. A month after that however there must have been more money available as further work was recorded including ten pairs of mittens to Grand Duke Michael's Appeal for aid to the Russian Army! There had been a letter of appreciation from Hospital ship Asturias in Southampton Docks. The retreat to the Marne and the fierce fighting which then followed at Ypres meant that many men had lost kit and possessions. As well as the work, significant sums of money continued to be raised. In May a list includes £40 for soldiers' garments and also £168 for the British Red Cross.

'Handkerchief Day' on 30 June when everyone was asked to bring one or more hankies (washed!) produced 840 handkerchiefs, from 168 people! In the same issue it was announced that the working party had recommenced to produce pyjamas and other hospital garments. In September it was noted that ten shirts and four pairs of socks had gone to a Belgian base hospital; 20 pairs of socks to the KRRC (Kings Royal Rifle Corps) at the front; ten suits of pyjamas, 20 pillows, 20 caps, and four nightshirts to Ambulance ships in the Dardanelles.

Through the rest of 1915 and into 1916 there continued to be lists of clothing sent and their destinations, with letters of thanks from various recipients. It seems clear that the demand was great and the decisions as to where to send what was produced must have been difficult. From July 1915 to May 1916, 702 items had been sent, including a further 406 handkerchiefs. At this time the Parish Magazine noted two momentous events, the Battle of the Somme, and the death of Lord Kitchener.

In August 1916 there is the first notice of a War Hospital Depot which had opened at Freelands in Shawford in October 1915. Although this is in Shawford I feel that many in Twyford must have been involved for it to be mentioned in the Twyford Parish Magazine. This depot was for the production of hospital supplies, dressings etc. In the time between its opening and this mention, 34,448 items of hospital supplies had been sent off. Some of the replies of thanks are quoted such as; 'Rouen hospital working 18 hours a day, we want anything, can you help us?' In January 1918 a Rummage sale for 'the Twyford and Shawford Hospital Supplies Depot raised just under £100.' It was commented that this however will not go very far; 'prices have increased a lot, Gauze which was lately nine shillings a roll is now 15 shillings.' In June 1918 a house to house collection raised £278 11s 5d. With thanks for everyone's generosity, praise is given for 'even small amounts from those who have little to spare.'

Shawford & Twyford, Hospital Supply Depot.

In today's terms it does seem extraordinary that basic items such as clothing, pyjamas and more especially hospital dressings should have been so dependent on voluntary efforts. I have no information on what the government provided, but one has to assume that it was not adequate. The generosity of the village is remarkable.

In July 1915 there is the first mention of a voluntary scheme for supplying fresh fruit and vegetables to the Royal Navy at sea. Deputy Inspector General Anderson RN who lived in the village was appointed the local representative of a national scheme. 'The Admiralty does not include these items, except for potatoes, in its regular rations and men at sea are dependent upon private gifts... and I will receive and send any offerings if sent to Roman Villa on Monday mornings as early as possible.' Those donors who could send a crate already packed are asked to send it to Mr Arthur Smith at the Brewery Buildings. As with the clothing and hospital supplies it does seem an extraordinary demand. The cause of scurvy had been well known for a long time and I imagine that ships at sea did issue lime juice, (British sailors were known as Limeys for that reason). Adequate cold storage for perishable vegetables was probably very limited, but the Home Fleet with its various squadrons around the coast must have been able to return to base regularly for supplies. In September, a letter from J H Anderson thanks the inhabitants of Twyford for contributing in kind and in money to this 'grand scheme for providing such an absolute necessity for our sailors in the North Sea Fleet'. The committee was making every arrangement for sending out what a generous public was providing and there was evidence of the good effect this was having on the men's health. Nearly 100 parcels had been dispatched from Twyford weighing a very large amount. It is intended to carry on with this work for our sailors during the war with a weekly collection.

December 1915 was the end of the first year of the scheme and the average weekly national supply had been 2,700 packages weighing 270,000 pounds. Twyford was the first place in Hampshire to form a branch, one of eventually 42 branches. There had been difficulties with funding packages, the railways offered free carriage but it was difficult to get boxes returned etc. By April 1916 the contributions had obviously dropped and Inspector General Anderson suggests that 'the inhabitants do not sufficiently appreciate what the nation owes to the Navy, or if they do are not grateful enough.'! This is fairly powerful stuff and I have to say that to me it sounds unfair and tactless. I suspect that after almost two years of war with heavy losses of men, people generally did not need this sort of reminder of the efforts needed.

Later in the year there was talk of getting a dedicated plot of land for growing vegetables for this cause but it did not work out. In June Inspector General Anderson is complaining again; 'he has seen quantities of broccoli and sprouting greens in gardens and allotments going to waste.' And he urges everyone to not fail and send all that they are able to spare.

In November 1916 J H Anderson reported that the Daily Graphic newspaper had taken up this subject, and made another appeal for help, suggesting that the village is not doing enough. In May 1917 contributions dropped again following some severe weather, but in August, although he records a large list of items, he again has a go at the village saying that contributions had dropped to a minimum and he lambasts those who 'have apparently forgotten how much we are indebted to the Navy', and appeals again for more generous help. I think he is ungenerous in his comments as he compares Twyford unfavourably with other nearby villages which send such 'large consignments'. His diatribes have irritated me as I have read through the magazines and I wonder how the people in the village felt. This seems to be the last of Inspector General Anderson's reports although there is still over a year to go before the end of the war.

Finally, another area of voluntary help with food supplies was with the introduction of the National Egg Collection. This was first recorded in February 1916 with a mention that Twyford's egg collection had produced 2,828 eggs. These had been sent to various hospitals and to a central depot in London. Mrs Pearson of Orchard Close thanks 'all the kind friends who have helped her to achieve such a good result.' In June 1917 there is another note about this collection. In May, the organising secretary had called at the school asking to establish a depot for the collection and despatch of eggs from Twyford for army use, particularly at base hospitals in France. The National Scheme had already collected and sent off 30 million eggs, 17 million of which had been collected through elementary schools. Older children act as collectors with Society badges. Both boys and girls are very keen indeed, and nearly all children bring an egg to school with them every week which they have bought with their pocket money. There is one further mention in May 1918 with a report of more eggs sent off plus a donation of £41 12s 5d.

This is a brief account of Twyford's activities to support the war effort, taken from the pages of the Parish Magazines, which, in spite of the comments of Inspector General Anderson, seem to me to reveal a great and continuing generosity in the village associated with a lot of hard work and organisation. There is a lot of patriotic sentiment in the pages although there must have been a war-weariness towards the end.

Bruce Lees

Hazeley Down Camp

Hazeley Down rises north-east of the village of Twyford, where the ground gently slopes up to the parish boundary with Morestead, rising from about 30 metres in the village to over a hundred metres above sea level. The Hazeley Road runs along the foot of the down to a T-junction on the Morestead Road, which at this point follows the Roman Road, from Silchester to Portchester on the coast, via Winchester. Beyond Hazeley the ground continues to rise to Fawley Down and Cheesefoot Head giving fine views to Southampton and the coast. There is plenty of open country offering suitable terrain for military training and there are rifle ranges there to this day.

The Hazeley Down Camp was one of seven on the downs around Winchester. They were major training and embarkation points, feeding troops into the transport system down to the docks at Southampton and on to France. The others were three camps at Morn Hill; Winnall Down, Magdalene Hill and Avington. There were further camps at Pitt Corner, Olivers Battery/Badger Farm, Flowerdown Camp at Littleton and Worthy Down Camp. Hursley also had a large camp and hospital. All were new camps created for the war and were substantial, what we know of Hazeley Down applied generally to the others, a particular attraction of Hazeley doubtless being Twyford Waterworks less than a mile away. As the plans for the camps took shape, the War Department (WD) requisition for some 105 acres of the Down reached John Best, he had only completed his purchase of Hazeley Farm in 1914.[1]

What came to be Hazeley Down Camp included barracks, stables, veterinary facilities, a hospital and facilities for the troops, including a barbers, post office, banks and shops and the renowned YMCA hut.

The Camp Store circa 1917, opposite the footpath to the Memorial, and today

The local area also provided training areas and rifle ranges. Construction had begun in February 1915, was completed in October 1915 and for much of its life the place was colloquially known as "Mud Down". The barrack huts offered three-plank bunks 'upholstered' with straw mattresses. Very quickly the huts became rat-infested. The scale of the place can be gauged from one of four sale particulars for Hazeley Down Camp provided by Gudgeons Auctioneers when the camps were sold off after the war. In just this one sale, there were 80 barrack huts, eight bath houses, 44 ablution huts and latrines and 77 miscellaneous buildings. The camp could accommodate 6,500 men (four times the population of Twyford at that time) and stabling for 1,500 horses, five miles of road had been laid to service the buildings with 3.5 miles of drains and 13 miles of electric cabling. The men and horses needed 95,000 gallons of water per day.

The place was used by a range of troops, units from the 38th Welsh Division, The Royal Newfoundland Regiment, Portuguese Artillery and Infantry, by some accounts "White Russians", the Royal Garrison Artillery, 24th Officer Cadet Battalion (Tank Corps), and of course the London Regiments. Following the deployment of the 38th Welsh Division to France in November/December 1915 the camp appears to be occupied by reserve units acting as casualty replacements for battalions and regiments deployed on active service. Many did their 13 and a half week basic training at the camp, while others would have been there for a relatively short time. These were concentrated into drafts of platoon strength and were sent to Flanders as reinforcing troops, boarding trains at Shawford Station for their onward journey.

The later sculptor Rifleman Henry Moore did his training here with the Civil Service Rifles and war poet Wilfred Owen had cause to visit his cousin, Leslie Gunston, who was carrying out his On War Service work at the camp YMCA. Owen spent the night at Hazeley and served coffee to the troops at the YMCA the following morning.

While the existence of the camp today is betrayed by the tree-planting visible from the Morestead Road, indicating the layout of the site, the most significant memorial is the Wayside Cross by the footpath running North/South on the Western edge of the Camp. This bears the names of the London battalions which spent time there:-

13TH BATTN. LONDON REGT. (KENSINGTONS)
14TH BATTN. LONDON REGT. (LONDON SCOTTISH)
15TH BATTN. LONDON REGT. (CIVIL SERVICE)
16TH BATTN. LONDON REGT. (QUEEN'S WESTMINSTER RIFLES)
17TH BATTN. LONDON REGT. (POPLAR & STEPNEY RIFLES)
20TH BATTN. LONDON REGT. (BLACKHEATH & WOOLWICH).

The London Regiments' Wayside Cross at Hazeley Down

On the 30 July 1916 a memorial service, attended by some 5,000 officers and men, was held at Hazeley Down Camp, to commemorate the men of the London Regiments killed to that point in the war, a measure of the shock and grief felt by so many at a point when there was no end yet in sight. At the time of the service it was decided to allocate part of the memorial service fund to the more permanent memorial to the fallen men of the London Regiments in the form of the wayside cross mentioned. The cross was designed by Rifleman Norman Keep of the Queens Westminster Rifles, made by Mr G Blackwell of Winchester, and later erected on the site at Hazeley Down Camp.

Memorial Service of the London Battalions - 30 July 1916

The Royal Garrison Artillery also made a significant mark, cutting their cap-badge into the Down at the entrance to the camp, reinforcing it with concrete later. Sadly it does not survive.

There appear to have been quite close relations between the camp and the village, even though the size of the camp substantially outweighed the village and the camp had been designed to be self-sufficient, with its own shop and recreation facilities. The village would have been aware of arrivals and departures as bodies of troops marched from the station, across the cross-roads and down the Hazeley Road to their new home. Thereafter soldiers came into the village, doubtless for a drink and for the occasional event at the Parish Hall, there are records of these going on to two o'clock, am! We know that Private Hooton of the London Scottish took a lively interest in the boys of the Bible Class, instructing them in gym and PT. Church services were attended by men from the camp and, sadly, two deaths at the camp resulted in burials in St Mary's Churchyard.

Following the signing of the Armistice on 11 November 1918 the camps surrounding Winchester, including Hazeley Down, became repatriation camps for overseas troops and holding camps for UK troops awaiting discharge.

Finally, once all the troops had gone, the camp buildings and their contents were to be sold at auctions between January 1920 and September 1921 and, in the case of Hazeley Down, the land returned to agriculture. There was a last minute move to retain the significant contribution to the infrastructure stock that the camp represented. On 7 December 1920 Colonel Sir John Newman, MP for Finchley, asked the Minister of Health in the House

> *"whether he is aware that an unoccupied hutment camp at Hazeley Down, near Twyford, is being dismantled although it has the water laid on, a perfect drainage system, expensive new roads, and many garden plots laid out, and would therefore provide housing accommodation at a cost very much below that required to build cottages which are proposed;. whether, in the interests of housing or of public economy, this demolition will not be proceeded with*

while labourers in the neighbourhood are anxious to occupy these huts, which could be converted into bungalows at a cost not exceeding £150; and whether he is aware that this demolition has been authorised for the purpose of finding employment for certain unemployed men?"[2]

However this move would have required significant further legal processes, the requisition which applied to Hazeley would simply unwind when the WD occupation ceased, the land was never bought or conveyed to the WD. So the demolition proceeded, with the land being returned to the Best family, although many of the buildings were salvaged, finding new uses in the surrounding district as school buildings, village halls, farm buildings, workshops, miscellaneous housing and some still survive, eg our former scout hut next to the Parish Hall, bought in the May 1920 Gudgeon Sale by a couple for their son's chemistry lab and later donated to the village for community use.

Christopher Pope, with thanks to Patrick Craze.

References:

1. "Twyford Ringing The Changes", Doreen Pearce and Stanley Crooks, George Mann Publications, Nov 1999 - ISBN 0-95-244243-4, pages 145, 157, et al.
2. Hansard Minute, HC Deb 07 December 1920, vol 135 c1942W1942W.

View of the Camp, 1915

The First Winter at Hazeley Down Camp

Royal Garrison Artillery enjoying a cup of tea at the camp

Portuguese Troops Settling in at the Camp

YMCA Hut – Hazeley Down Camp

Twyford Bells – Their Message

"While standing in Compton Tunnel (which the Glosters are guarding) on Sunday evening, the ringing of the Twyford church bells brought thoughts into the mind of the writer, which are embodied in the following verses:-

Twyford village bells are ringing
Cross the meadows, music flinging
Sweetly sound their notes are winging
Like the seagulls rise and fall.
And I hear them gently pealing
With a reverential feeling
As they o'er my senses stealing
So melodiously call.

But the sterner note is ringing
And a message, keen and stinging
Into every heart is dinging
Of a duty and a will.
And a nation's soul is waking
Hearth and home and loves forsaking
With manhood in the making
Soon to rise, though some must fall.

Once again will bells be ringing
And the women will be singing
To the marching and the swinging
Of the lads behind the gun.
Then will come again the gladness
Born in turmoil and of sadness
Of a nation's fight with madness
Of a victory nobly won.

Corporal F J Carter, 2/5th Battalion Glosters

Winchester, January 11th 1916"

6. AFTERWORD - Impact on the Village

By 1918 the village must have been truly weary of war. But already people were beginning to think about commemoration and post-conflict rebuilding. In 1917 the Imperial War Graves Commission, now of course the Commonwealth War Graves Commission, was established by Royal Charter to manage the graves and formally remember every British and Empire serviceman who died in the war. Land within their territories had already been granted to the UK by the French and Belgian governments 'in perpetuity' for use as graves and cemeteries. Also in 1917 the Government was developing its plans for design of a Memorial Plaque for presentation to the families who had lost loved ones and in March 1918 the winning design was announced; an example can be seen in our article on Thomas Knight.

Back in Twyford people were also considering commemoration. In the Parish Magazine for September 1918, the Reverend C T Wickham raised the question of a memorial to commemorate the fallen and was suggesting ideas for the form this might take. His plan was to erect a Lych-Gate at the north entrance to the Churchyard, but he also suggested filling of the west window with "good stained glass", extending and improving the Churchyard, whilst allowing for a wide consultation to "secure the thoroughly representative approval of any scheme before it is adopted."

The following month Athol Maudslay wrote candidly that "a lych-gate does not appeal to me: such lych-gates as I have seen have always seemed a waste of labour and material, fulfilling no commensurate purpose. Besides a lych-gate would obstruct the view, ...". Maudslay then went on to describe his own pet scheme to rectify the perceived blunder of the architect in his design of the chancel steps. But he did include another suggestion, perhaps guiding people towards what was to prove the eventual solution, proposing "Then again beneath the west window there should be a memorial tablet, white marble on a polished granite plinth, upon which should be inscribed the names of all the Twyford men and boys ...".

The following month Harold Morris called for suggestions and proposed a public meeting at which all ideas could be considered. In the same edition Morris recounted how Miss Campbell, the loss of whose brother Bruce was recorded on the same page, had written to him suggesting "an oak screen, with a list of every man from the village ...".

In the November edition, the end of the war was recorded in a single modest paragraph:

> *"On Monday, November 11' the armistice was signed with Germany. The war is over. We have come through to victory. What can we say but "Glory be to thee O Lord Most High."*

Not so much a trump as a palpable sigh of relief.

In successive months further ideas for the memorial appeared.

On Wednesday 5 February 1919, the proposed meeting to take the matter forward took place. I think we can assume it was a big one. A total of twelve ideas were recorded for consideration and, in fact, another one was proposed in a late letter to the magazine editor. The outcome was to select a committee to make the final choice. From this distance the composition of the committee was a genuine attempt to achieve a consensus on what looked as though it could become a thorny problem with so many pet schemes being canvassed. In all a total of 24 people were appointed to serve, including former servicemen, ladies from the WI and others, Miss Hull, Parish and PCC Councillors; several names from the bereaved families appeared.

Despite the initial range of views about the form of the memorial, the committee's deliberations resulted in the dignified panelling we can see today and it was installed in 1921. The cost for it was amply met by widespread subscription within the village.

An additional record was maintained in the village of all the men who had served overseas in the course of the war. There are 170 names on the two boards in the Parish Hall, listed in the appendix below. These show 116 different family names with 37 appearing more than once, suggesting that two to four members of the same family had served. Bear in mind that this was not the total who answered the call, as it would have excluded those retained for home service, any called up and then discharged, etc. However employing the statistic that 9.5 approx younger men moved into the age group each year, we can quantify the impact of the war on the village's menfolk as follows:

Total Twyford males aged 18 – 38 in 1914 (approx)	184
Four further 'years-worth' (9.5 x 4)	38
Total Twyford males aged 18 – 38, over the war years	228
Coarse proportion of Twyford men who served abroad	
170/228 *100	75%

Thus it would appear that a very significant 75% of Twyford's military age males were deployed abroad in the course of the war, expressed another way, 25% of the entire male population. Allowing for the considerations Chris Corcoran points out in Chapter 1, the unfit, mis-counting males from neighbouring villages, etc, the proportion of the village's menfolk in uniform was very substantial. These figures changed the village for a century, as they have our national life. Looked at from another perspective, this village had contributed enormously to wartime manpower demands, had the conflict continued for significantly longer Twyford could not have been able to continue its response, the tank was nearing empty.

The 29 men and boys commemorated on our memorial were a varied lot. Although the average age was 26, there were very young and old. Two 16 year-olds and one only 17, in all eleven 20 or under. There were nine 21 - 30, and a further nine 30-year-olds, two in their 40s and one aged 53. Although the majority died in action, KIA 15, six Died of Wounds and a further six of Illness and Disease, a total of twelve, many of whom might have survived given more modern medical developments. I suppose inevitably there were accidents, three lost to this cause, in addition to one suicide and one from Natural Causes. [The records suggest that at least one of the KIA figures was a victim of what we would nowadays call 'friendly fire', but the war diaries may have been reluctant to tackle this classification comprehensively.] Our men fought all over the world and are buried where they fell, twelve in France, five in Belgium, two at sea and one each in Greece, India, Italy and Turkey, the remainder in England.

Whilst we might think of Twyford as a stable rural and agricultural parish, the birthplaces of the men confirm the mobility of people at this time. Only seven were born in Twyford, although 12 hailed from less than 20 miles away, while ten were born all over, from Binfield to Bolton, Dorset and London to Essex and the Punjab. However by 1911 twenty-three of the twenty-nine were living in or connected to Twyford, Colden Common and Winchester, the remainder were in England and two were in India. Within the village, their families were spread around. The homes of five were on the High Street, four lived in Queen Street, two at Hockley and/or North Town and the others at St Mary's Terrace, Park Lane, Roman Road, Hazeley, Brambridge and Shawford.

The multiplicity of their pre-war occupations is surprising. Working from the 1911 census, the largest single occupation was 'regular serviceman', two sailors and four soldiers, thereafter gardeners came in with six, two of whom worked for Twyford School, agriculture two, grooms two and a wagoner. Two could be described as working in motor/engineering, there were two butchers, two salesmen, a footman, a waterworks stoker, a gas works labourer, a carpenter and a telegraph messenger boy, and of course three were at school.

In a few cases their connection with the village was slight, parents moving into the village during or even shortly after the war clearly established a connection that had to be respected. What seems to be the case is that inclusion on the Twyford memorial was not restrictive, any man or bereaved family with a village connection both before and after the war was included on the Roll of Honour.

War weary though the village was in the spring of 1920, and weary of the endless fund-raising, sacrifices and drip-feed of bad news, the lasting human cost of the war for Twyford was counted in terms of 25 families bereaved, 11 war widows, nine orphaned children and twenty-nine names on wooden boards at the back of church.

7. APPENDICES

Twyford's Roll of Honour

This a direct transcription of the names on the boards shown at Chapter 2.

No.	Inscription
1	Chas Frederick MUSSELL Pte Hants Regt 1914
2	William LIGHT Pte Manchester Regt 1914
3	Lennox Dutton SHRIMPTON Cpl Grenadier Guards 1914
4	Frederick Robt BROWN Pte Hants Regt 1915
5	Walter George WEBB Sergt Wiltshire Regt 1915
6	Mark WEBB Stoker 1st Class Torpedo Boat no 96 1915
7	Leonard H A HERRIDGE Cpl Ontario Regt 1915
8	Frank Henry J DUMPER Pte Hants Regt 1915
9	Geo Rainier CRAWFORD CB Colonel D. of Wellingtons Regt 1915
10	Jack Stanley POWELL Pte Hants Regt 1915
11	Thomas Mostyn FIELD Midshipman HMS Queen Mary 1916
12	Walter Chas C. COX Pte Hants Regt 1916
13	Geo William HADLEY L-Cpl Hants Regt 1917
14	Edwin PLATT Captain Winnipeg Rifles 1917
15	George MANSELL Pte Dorset Regt 1917
16	Walter Chas H. FELTHAM Sergt Hants Regt 1917
17	Wm James BARNES Pte Dorset Regt 1917
18	George COLLINS Pte Royal Irish Fusiliers 1917
19	Walter SHAVE Pte Worcestershire Regt 1917
20	Bruce Hutchinson CAMPBELL Lieut Gordon Highlandrs 1918
21	Herbert Tring SAPSED Cpl RNAS 1918
22	Albert Chas HICKMAN Cpl RASCMT 1918
23	Sydney A MUSSELL Sergt Hants Regt 1918
24	Henry P PARROTT Pte Lincolnshire Regt 1918
25	William EADES Pte MGC 1918
26	Thomas Wm KNIGHT Pte Devon Regt 1918
27	Percy F J ALLEN Gunner RHA 1919
28	Ernest REASON Staff Sergt RASC 1919
29	Alfred J HIGGINS 10th Hants

Contributors to the Project

Mike Andrews
Steve Bailey
Jane Beljic
Michael Biddle
Susie Biddle
Andrew Brooks
Chris Corcoran
Vanessa Croucher
Vicki Dunlop
Andrew Keeling
Sue Kennedy
Bruce Lees
Barbara Mansell
Brian Matthews
Jeff Mardon
Colin Oram
David Owen
Rosanna Perkin
Christopher Pope
Ralph Scaiff
David Snoswell
Jeremy Thoday

Particular thanks also to:

Patrick Craze	Hazeley Down Camp
Rachel Holmes	The Hampshire Regiment Museum and Archives, Serles House
Bernard Sullivan	Parish Registers
Graham Hill	Photographs and access to Miss Hull's Album
Andrew Pope	Land Management
Vicki Dunlop	Tireless Sub Editor and Picture Editor

Parish Hall Boards

1914 MEN OF TWYFORD WHO SERVED ABROAD IN THE GREAT WAR 1918

F Abraham
A Allen
J W H Ambrose
W R Annals
R L Baker
W Baker
J Barnard
A Berner
W Brightman
F Budd
J C Bull
W Bundy
F Burfitt
F Cannings
W Cavell
C E Cawte
J Cloke
E Cobb
F Coleman
R Coleman
W Conduct
W Cooke
F Cousins
W Cousins
W S Cowland
H Dangerfield
A Day
S Day
W Day
F Dicks
T Dicks
J Dowse
G P L Drake-Brockman
H E Drake-Brockman
A E Drew
F Dunbar
H Eaton
G E Edmonds
J T Elkins
J J Elliott
H Fabian
W Fancy
F Fidler
W Foard
C G Found
F E Found
F W Found
J Fraser
J Froud
H Garratt
L W Gilbert
G H Gilbey
O S Gilbey
H V Gillett
G Guile
S J Guppy
E Hadley
F Hadley
H Hadley
J Hadley
C Haines
G Hamilton
W Harrison
C Harvey
W Hawkins
H Herage
L Herage
W Herridge
A Hickman
J Hickman
C Hobbs
H Hodgson
E Howells
C Hubbard
A Ings
A Jannaway
B Jetton
H Jetton
S Jetton
A Johnson
F Johnson
F Josland
A Laishley
H Laishley
A Lampard
L Lampard
A Lawrence
L Light
W Light
P Long
B Longman
A Mansbridge
W Mansbridge
F Mansell
G Mansell
L Marriner
L Martin
S Martin
A Matthews
F Matthews
H Matthews
F Money
A Morris
G S Morris
J Neville
W Neville
W Newell
F Oxenbury
C Oxford
T Oxford
J Padwick
G Page
H Page
F J Parker
P Parrott
F Passingham
J Peadon
W Pearcy
J Plummer
J R Pounce
H Redman
P Redman
A Reynolds
F Reynolds
C M Roberts
G Ruby
A Sapsed
W Sapsed
G Sawkins
J Sawkins
D Saywell
W Saywell
W Shadwell
G Sharp
R Sherfield
A J Smith
B Smith
E Smith
F T Smith
H Smith
S Smith
A Steele
J Steele
A Stewart
A Stratton
A H Stratton
A Talmage
H Trent
A Unsworth
A Wakely
G Wakely
L Walker
R Walker
R Walker
C Wallis
C Wateridge
E Wateridge
W Wateridge
H Watts
R Watts
W Webb
R West
A White
F White
G White
G White
P White
R White
W White
F A Yorke

Bible Class Roll of Honour

St. Mary's Bible Class.

Roll of Honour

DURING THE GREAT WAR, 1914—1919.

Frank Dumper, Hampshire Regt. (Died in Hospital in India)
Jack S. Powell, Hampshire Regt. (Died in Hospital in England)
W. Charles C. Cox, Hants. Regt. (Killed in Action in France).
George Collins, R. Irish Fus. (Killed in Action in France)
Sidney A. Mussell, Hants. Regt. (Killed in Action in France)
Frank Hunt, Hampshire Regt. (Killed in Action in France)
Tom W. Knight, Devonshire Regt. (Killed in Action in France)
H. Peter Parrott, Lincs. Regt. (Died of Wounds in France)
Percy F. G. Allen, R.H.A. (Died in Hospital in England)

William Price, Hampshire Regt.
Alfred Mansbridge, R.A.S.C.
Ernest Hadley, Hampshire Regt.
Fredk. Found, Devon. Regt. (wounded)
Harold Watts, Hampshire Regt.
Ernest Drew, Hampshire Regt.
Charles Cawte, Hants. Regt. (wounded)
Walter Cook, R.N., H.M.S. Repulse
William Harrison, R.A.S.C.
Tom Oxford, Hants. Regt. (wounded)
Lewis Walker, R. Engineers (wounded)
William Sapsed, Hants. Regt. (wounded)
Sidney Boyes, Royal Navy.
Arthur Stratton, Worc. Regt. (wounded)
Arthur Smith, Royal Warwicks.

Edward Sawkins, Royal Engineers
Cyril Laishley, Hampshire Regt.,
Robert Hickman, Royal Air Force.
Reginald Miles, Royal Air Force.
Fred Unsworth, Royal Air Force.
Fred Hadley, Royal Marines. L.I.
Albert H. Stratton, Hants. Regt.
Charles Wateridge, Worc. Regt.
Geoffrey Stevens, Royal Air Force.
Archie Jannaway, Royal Warwicks.
Walter Watkins, Dorset R. (wounded)
Percy Parrott, Glouc. R. (wounded)
Leonard Parrott, Royal Air Force.
Stanley Trent, 1st King's R. Rifles.
Frank Radley, Royal Marines L.I.

Photograph Acknowledgements

Photographs and illustrations are drawn from both local and nationally available sources. The copyright of many new photographs has been vested by the photographers in St Mary's Parochial Church Council. Illustrations are identified by page number. Any errors or omissions from this list should be notified to the publisher.

5, 6, 43, 60, 95, 100, 105, 134, 160, 164, 166, 167, 169, 170 & 171 from Graham Hill's Collection; 39, Miss Hull courtesy of Ingrid Percival; 58 from Graham Hill's Collection and courtesy of Molly Emmett; 10, 11, 39, 63, 70, 103, 110, 122, 125, 143, 146, 148, 153, 155, 165 & back cover Courtesy of Twyford St Mary's Parochial Church Council; 19, Courtesy of Nottingham City Council Photographic Archive; 24, British Army WWI Medal Rolls Index Cards, 1914-1920 ex Ancestry.com.; 32, 38, 61, 76, 112 & 142 from Miss Hull's Photo Album; 43, 74 Courtesy of The Commonwealth War Graves Commission; 49, Courtesy of Mellors and Kirk, The Auction House, Gregory St, Nottingham; 48, Courtesy of Dr and Mrs Richard Fry; 50, George Clausen 1890; 55, Courtesy of Adrian Vicary, The Maritime Photo Library; 56, Courtesy of Tyne and Wear Museums; 57, The Graveyard Detective (http://graveyarddetective.
blogspot.com/); 61, From Miss Hull's Photo Album; 65 & 127 Courtesy of Twyford School, Winchester, Hampshire; 65, 127 Courtesy of Twyford School archive; 66, Image is used by the kind permission of Stanley Gibbons Ltd.; 69, 94 & 116 ex www.wikipedia.org; 76, From Miss Hull's Photo Album; 80, Courtesy of the Imperial War Museum photograph (Q53602); 83, Courtesy of City of Southampton Archives; 85, Ancestry.com, Internet; 86, Courtesy of The Twyford Waterworks Trust; 108, Courtesy of the Imperial War Museum photograph (Q3995); 117, ex internet, http://www.theobservationpost.com/blog/?p=521; 118, Courtesy of Joan Freemantle; 121, Courtesy of Michael W. Pocock and www.MaritimeQuest.com; 122, Courtesy of the Sapsed Family; 128 ex eBay; 130, Reproduced from The Story of the Salonica Army, by G Ward Price, New York, Edward J. Clode, 1918, appears also on Wikipedia.; 140, Courtesy of the Reason Family; 155, http://www.workhouses.org.uk/Alresford/; 171, Courtesy of the Imperial War Museum (Q 30097).

Map of Twyford in 1910

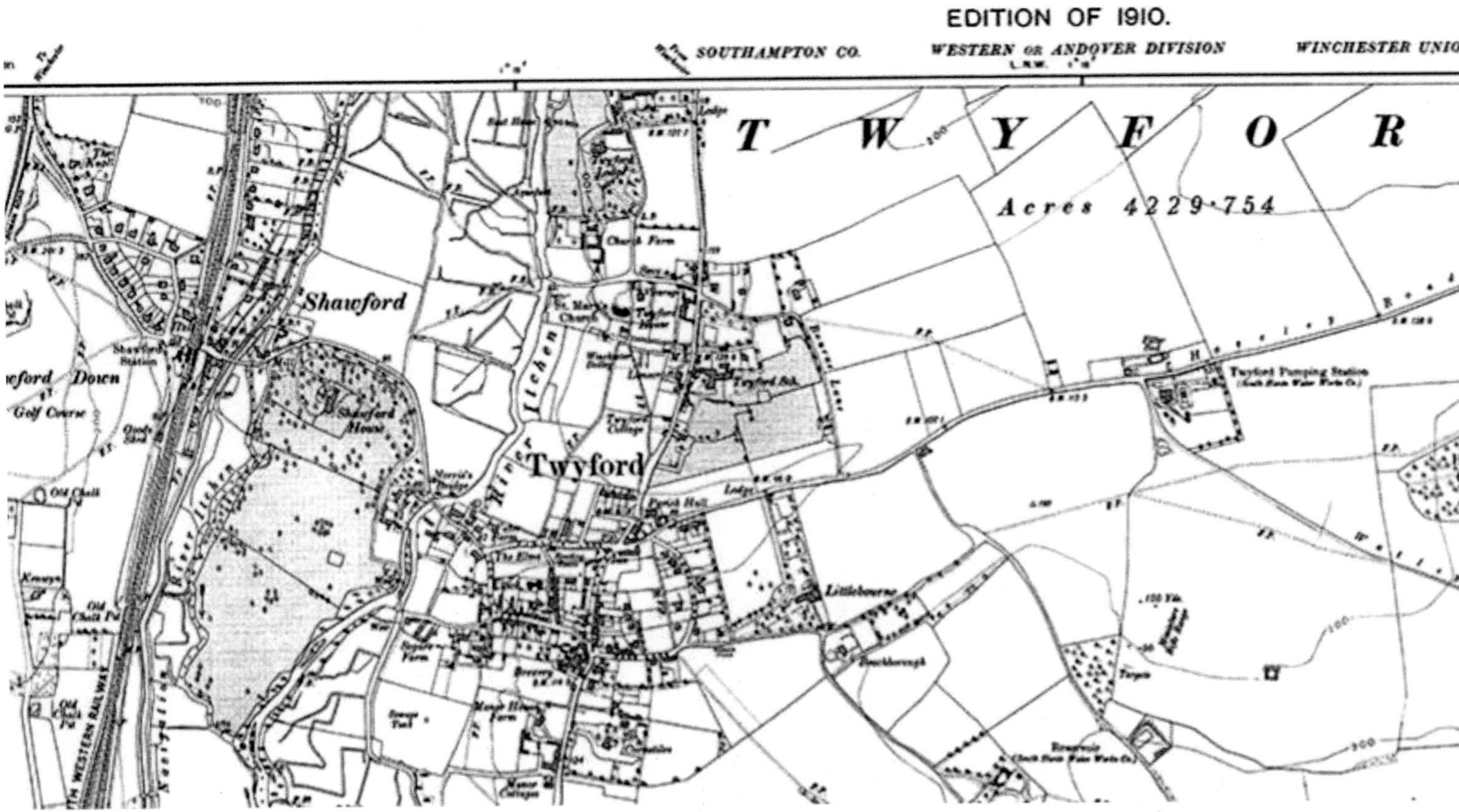